Lee Wessman

Notebook

*One Man's Take on Life, Love
and Costa Rican Pizza*

Published by the
Sacramento Business Journal
1401 21st Street, Suite 200
Sacramento, California 95814

ISBN 0-9725401-0-5
Printed in the United States of America

This book has been assembled by the staff of the
Sacramento Business Journal.
Editors: Dan Kennedy and Bill Buchanan
Production editor and graphic designer: Jay Leek
Back cover photo by Dennis McCoy

To order more copies of this book,
please call the Sacramento Business Journal at
916.447.7661

Table of Contents

"Footsyball"
Sharks, Intolerance and Making Life Work

"A Two-Tailed Crawdad? Really?"
Of Sports, Skiing, Work and Life in the Sun

Foreword

For 16 years, Lee Wessman wrote newspaper columns that had an enormous following. He did it in a relatively small city – Sacramento, California – and his material was the simple stuff of life.

His words always resonated with people, whether his subject was surfing with sharks, home construction projects that went awry, or the more memorable moments that came his way as the father of two daughters. People wondered when his most enduring pieces would be collected in a book, which they could mail off to relatives or give to colleagues and neighbors.

I always assumed he'd be around to help with that task, whenever we got organized enough to do it. But a brain aneurysm struck him down in February 2002, at age 47.

I've been the publisher of the Sacramento Business Journal, where Lee oversaw an accomplished news staff and won awards as editor, for all of those 16 years. Yet the work he would be remembered for, we all knew, were the personal Notebooks he wrote late on Wednesday nights, when the newsroom was otherwise deserted. The next morning, the new edition would be off to the printer. Deadlines and darkness seemed to harness all his powers to tell a story.

The following for his Notebooks grew to include readers from far-flung cities because his tales have universal appeal. For example, there was the one about the time, as a much younger man, when the driver's side door of his dilapidated Econoline van broke open on a sharp turn. He spilled from the driver's seat to the pavement, where he had a fine view of what happened next. He needed all his story-telling skills to make something up for the police.

Ordinary people on vacation in Hawaii spend their week in a hotel or a condo. Lee and Kelli, his wife, nosed about the islands until they found a remote tropical spot where their two very young girls, Rachel and Lauren, could swim with wild dolphins in a quiet sea and sleep in hammocks in the open air.

I remember the day Lee returned from a trip to Costa Rica, where he surfed for hours on a beach where he could see big sharks in the clear ocean. He'd grown up surfing with sharks; it wouldn't drive him to shore, even though he'd had some close encounters.

He had a "playful, sometimes wicked, sense of humor," in the words of one reader. Another told me, "I would read every word Lee Wessman wrote, often laughing or wiping away a tear at the end. His columns were my guilty pleasure in the office."

Personally, I could easily be persuaded that Lee somehow had a genetic link with Mark Twain, another journalist who once toiled for a Sacramento newspaper. Both men mined the same rich vein of material, pointing out ironies, making people laugh, and telling grand tales. Being politically correct had not the slightest interest to either man, except to the extent that correctness provided wonderful opportunities to turn something on its ear.

The French speak of terroir, a high-falutin' word that Lee would never use. It's the notion that something – wine or food usually – shows the flavor of the place it comes from. The concept holds true, in a similar way, as you consider the sensibilities of this talented writer. He lived on a mountainside outside Placerville, a community known during the California Gold Rush as Hangtown, and was also active in local theater and music circles. It's an irreverent place where an old-style American independence of spirit lives on. I find trace elements in all of Lee's Notebooks.

In closing, I can say with confidence that you will want to give this book to someone else. You'll want it back, but you'll want to share it first.

Be aware, though, that you may never see this book again, once it leaves your hands. The next person will want to share it too.

–Daniel Kennedy
August 23rd, 2002

For Kelli, Rachel and Lauren

I, Too, Was Stupid Once

Lessons From Home and Family

I, Too, Was Stupid Once

It was about 3 a.m. on a Saturday not so many months ago when I began to think about what a miracle it is that any male humans survive their teenage years.

A couple of boys whose families I know came softly tapping on my house. They were hoping to softly awaken my daughters. They also not-so-softly woke me.

The car they were driving had broken down on a remote road nearby. The car, I might add, that they were not supposed to be driving. Especially not at 3 a.m.

After threatening them with a chainsaw for trying to bring my kids into their caper, I tried to help them start the car. And when that didn't work, I took them home.

The question was whether I should wake their parents. I knew their folks were going to find out about the whole thing in the morning. They were majorly busted. But the boys begged me not to knock on the door.

What was more important: to break the news to their parents tonight, or to be a grown-up they could confide in?

I got to thinking about an incident when I was a kid. ...

... It is 1972. I am 18, living on my own now. My alarm goes off at 6 a.m. on a Monday – only a few hours after a Fleetwood Mac concert. I get up, scrape the hair off my tongue and manage to find my jeans and a T-shirt – but I can't find the keys to my '64 Chevy.

I wake up one of my roommates. "Rick, I can't find my keys and I gotta get to work. Can I borrow your van?"

Soon I have clambered into his Ford Econoline and am motoring along busy Beach Boulevard, slumped against the door as I steer the van.

I am not used to driving vans. But I don't give that much thought until, making a right turn at a crowded intersection, the right-front tire bumps into the curb.

And the door – which I am leaning against – pops open. And I pop out of the van.

The whole world goes into slow motion. I am suspended in mid-air, still in the sitting position. I land on my butt in the street – while the van keeps rolling.

It rolls ever so slowly – just fast enough so that I cannot jump up and catch it. It hops the curb, mows down an emergency call box belonging to the Huntington Beach Police Department, and keeps rolling.

And it rolls right smack into a 1965 Mustang sitting in the left turn lane.

I stand up. A young woman gets out of the car behind me. She is laughing hysterically. I look around. The intersection is full of people. They are all laughing.

The guy in the Mustang gets out. He is not laughing. He is look-ing at his car's badly crunched fender.

Now something takes over in me – some crude teenage survival mechanism.

I walk over, pick up the police call box, and proceed to hide it behind some pumps at the gas station on the corner – in full view of, what, 50 people?

Now I approach the guy with the Mustang, babbling that I'll pay for the damage to his car. OK, he says, got any insurance? Uh, no. OK, he says, how about a driver's license. I reach for my wallet. It is not there. Uh oh.

I do not look at his face as I scribble my address on paper bor-rowed from the hysterical laughing lady and promise to pay for his car.

Feeling suddenly bashful, I crank up the van as a motorcycle cop pulls up, cheeks bulging from beneath his helmet, and says in a drawl not native to the beach community, "I got a report of an auto accident heeere."

"No officer," I say, "no accident here."

And I drive away, dimly aware that 50 jaws have just dropped to the pavement in the intersection behind me.

I go park the van in the alley behind my apartment. No room-mates are home. So I go get some keys made for my own car. (Remember, this all began when I lost my keys.) And then, I blow off work and go surfing.

Later, I come home. Walking up to the front door I can hear a dozen of my friends inside, talking excitedly. When I enter, they all stop talking. Through clenched teeth my roommate Rick informs me that the police have towed away his van and issued a warrant for his arrest for hit-and-run driving – for mowing down a police call box and trying to hide it behind some gas pumps.

I go down to the police station and turn myself in. They lead me to a big, burly desk sergeant.

I start talking a mile a minute. It's not my roommate they want, I say – it's me. I was driving his van.

But! I say, the accident wasn't really my fault, because technically, I was not in the van at the time of the accident. I was sitting in the street. I was, in fact, more like an eyewitness to the whole thing.

I don't remember what I said about trying to hide the call box, except that my words came in a torrent.

For some reason, when I get done talking, this big, burly desk sergeant just says, "Kid, get out of here. We'll send you a bill for the call box."

And they did. It wound up costing me $700 (in 1972 dollars.) And the Mustang cost me $400. And fixing my roommate's van cost me $400.

Today, 30 years later, it still astonishes me that a desk sergeant in the Huntington Beach Police Department took pity on such a bone-head and set me free.

… And so at 3 a.m. on a Saturday not so many months ago, look-ing at those two pathetic, simpering, fearful boys in my pickup, I made my choice.

Angelique of the Strawberry Fields

Angelique was the one who got to us. She was four or five years old. Huge dark eyes in a scruffy face, with a smile that could melt rock.

She and her sister ran up to our car when we stopped to fill up with gas at a Pemex station. We were a couple of hundred miles down the Baja peninsula, in a farming community called San Quentin.

She was selling Chiclets. I knelt down to her level and, in my childlike Spanish, examined her inventory. "Rojo, y blanco y verde," I said, pointing to different colors of gum. "Si," she answered patiently, "rojo y blanco."

"Qual es su nombre? What's your name?"

"Angelique." She smiled bashfully.

My daughters leaned out the car window. "Would you like this?" asked Rachel, my oldest, offering a toy mermaid. "Por usted?"

Angelique's face burst into a blinding smile as she clutched the toy to her breast. My younger daughter, Lauren, held a teddy bear out to Angelique's sister. And now, all four children were beaming. I had never seen my children look so radiant.

When we had decided to go to Baja for spring break, my wife and I explained to the girls that they would see some beautiful scenery on this trip. But they would also see true poverty, the likes of which they had never seen.

All those times we told them to eat their dinner because there were poor kids out there going without – well, they were going to meet some of the kids we were talking about. We told them that we hoped they would come away understanding how fortunate they are.

They had responded in a way that makes a parent feel as if something has gone right. They went through their rooms and packed two big boxes of toys. We took the toys and our spare gas and our gear, and headed off to Baja.

We didn't know what we were looking for in this place of staggering contrasts. Endless, gorgeous coastlines – where raw sewage is dumped into the sea. Verdant, fertile fields – next to brown ones, where too many wells have made the groundwater salty. Robust prosperity next to grinding poverty.

There were welcoming smiles in the markets – smiles that thinly shrouded a growing resentment toward gringos from the north, where voters have said resoundingly that Mexicans are not welcome.

And there were strawberries, I might add. Big juicy strawberries that we bought and ate by the flat.

We didn't know what we were looking for when we came here, but it found us anyway. It found us now, with our trip nearing an end.

By now, giving away their toys had become the purpose of the trip, as far as my daughters were concerned. Everywhere, they found kids going without. They gave away their toys on the streets of Ensenada, on the remote beaches of El Socorro, and several times they insisted I go careening off the Transpeninsular highway so they could run out to hand some happily startled kid a toy.

The day Angelique and her sister ran up to our car was Rachel's 11th birthday.

It was the first time in her life Rachel had not received any presents for her birthday. A party had been promised instead, after the trip. We pulled together a makeshift cake, but that was it. Somehow, it didn't seem to matter to Rachel; she was preoccupied.

We watched Angelique and her sister run out of the Pemex station toward a shack down the road.

"She doesn't have any shoes!" Rachel exclaimed. Little Angelique was running barefoot across a rocky, glass-strewn roadside. My girls frantically dug in their bags and produced a pair of shoes. I paid for the gas and we drove up to where we had seen Angelique and her sister. We found them excitedly showing their new toys to their parents. Their mom and dad were a weathered couple of Mixteco Indians. They were in San Quentin to pick strawberries, cauliflower, tomatoes – the stuff we breeze into the supermarket and buy out of season all the time without thinking about where it comes from.

The stuff we gringos are no longer buying. Half of Baja's $10 million strawberry crop is rotting due to a U.S. hepatitis outbreak – even though no such outbreak has occurred in Mexico, and there's a strong possibility that the fruit was contaminated by a San Diego processor.

Families like Angelique's, field workers in Mexico, are paid $8 a day to harvest strawberries and move on. And $8 a day barely buys fish tacos for a family of four.

We offered Angelique the shoes. She took them with more joy than I can describe. And my 11-year-old had been given the most joyous and unforgettable birthday gift of her young life.

The eyes of Angelique's father met mine, and he saw that mine had misted over. He smiled sadly from somewhere deep down in the bittersweet place all parents save for those who show a generosity to our children that we wish we could afford to show ourselves.

How momentary our contribution to his family seemed. And how lasting was their contribution to mine.

Toy Shortages and Other Crises

I turn the lights out, kiss my children softly on their cheeks, and thank them as sweetly as I can for not wishing to have a Tickle Me Elmo.

It happens nearly every year at this time. A Great Christmas Marketing Emergency.

The year's most popular toy is all sold out. Film at 11 shows parents rushing the doors at department stores, grappling with each other, elbowing, kneeing, snarling, biting, battling – anything to avoid telling the kids that they aren't getting the gifts they really wanted.

Black markets develop so that parents can buy kids the stuff written – in blood – at the top of their Santa lists.

My wife and I have dodged the bullet. Our kids have never asked for a toy on the endangered species list.

They learned the hard way not to ask for toys they see in TV commercials. Because one year, that was what they got.

It was about five years ago. The girls were 4 and 5. 'Twas back in the days before homework, music lessons and Girl Scouts, when they still had time for TV.

They had fixated on a creature called My Baby Wah Wah Wah, or something like that.

She looked fantastic in the commercials. She crawled along the floor, sucking on a bottle of real milk. Then she tripped, skidded to a stop on her chin, and cried "wah wah wah" until a kid just like you picked her up and consoled her with hugs and kisses.

We didn't want to buy those things. We tried to talk them out of it. And when the girls were out of earshot, my wife and I nostalgically recalled when they were toddlers and asked Santa for simple things – things like Hamburger Helper, or brass door knockers.

But sure enough, when they made their lists for Santa that year, there it was, My Baby Wah Wah Wah.

Christmas came and they joyously opened the packages, only to discover that My Baby Wah Wah Wah was an annoying little Heinrich Himmler of a creature, hard as a rock to hug and mechanical as a Panzer tank in motion. And the featured "wah wah wah wah wah wah wah" had a screech like an air raid siren.

Within an hour, they hated My Baby Wah Wah Wah. We all did. And that was the last time I remember them requesting television toys for Christmas.

It appears I may never be the victim of a Great Christmas Marketing Emergency. It makes me a bit melancholy to think these risky days are nearly over.

My fifth-grader is trying to hold on to Santa Claus. She's surrounded by skeptics, but she's trying to believe.

Last weekend she asked point blank, "Dad, is there really a Santa? Tell me the truth."

And I thought back to when I was a kid.

I was not allowed to believe in Santa. My father told us, from an early age, that there was no such thing.

It had broken his heart when he was a boy, he explained, to find out the North Pole was only ice. And he didn't want us to get hurt in the same way, by believing in Santa.

I, however, chose not to believe Dad.

Surely, I thought, Dad is screwed up. His unhappy childhood robbed him of his faith in things bigger and more majestic than human beings.

So I went right on believing in Santa, the outlawed icon. It was my first blatant act of defiance.

Then there came the year of the Johnny Reb Cannon Great Christmas Marketing Emergency.

It was the year that tested my faith – in Santa, in Dad, in believing in anything.

I was 5 or 6, I think. For some reason that isn't clear to me now, I was a Civil War buff.

Maybe it was because I was living in a little civil war, right there in my own house.

Mom and Dad weren't getting along. For a while there, during summer, Dad had gotten his own apartment. They told us kids it was because he needed to be closer to work. But we knew jive when we heard it.

Then came November, and all of a sudden things were looking up. Dad had moved back in with us. Mom was smiling. And we went shopping for a brand new house. We would move in by Christmas.

Life was good again.

And that's when I asked for that Johnny Reb Cannon. The one on TV. A little cannon that fired plastic balls at your enemies. I put it on both of my lists – the one I gave Dad, and the list I didn't show him, for Santa.

The week before Christmas, it was time to move into the new house. We kids took the train with Mom to stay with grandparents. Dad stayed behind to move our stuff.

I didn't watch the evening news, so I didn't know what was going on – that a Great Christmas Marketing Emergency had been declared on Johnny Reb Cannons.

On Christmas Eve, we rode the train back home. Dad was waiting at the station to meet us. There was something wrong with the look on his face.

"I couldn't find one," he told me, lifting me into his arms. "They were all sold out. I couldn't find your cannon. I'm sorry, son."

Although my disappointment was powerful, it soon faded in the warmth of his arms.

But the look on his face – something was wrong with it, and I can still see it to this day.

That night, as I lay in bed listening for clandestine bells from a covert sleigh that I was not allowed to believe in, I heard shouts instead. Shouts, coming from the living room of our brand new house.

That was the night their marriage finally ended.

Dad was gone in the morning. He never stayed another night with us in that house or any other house.

I learned there are worse things that can happen than a Great Christmas Marketing Emergency. And I never asked for another one of those damned TV toys, either.

Now my daughter asks me if Santa is real. And I have no choice but to tell her the truth.

"You bet he is, honey," I say. "But not everybody is wise enough to believe. He only exists for those of us who know how to believe.

"Now, let's fill out your list."

Inch by Inch They Earn Their Wings

Twenty-three barefoot orphans shuffle anxiously. An orchestra strikes up. The kids count under their breath – one measure, two measures – and in a burst of song they take the stage.

It is opening night for the community theater production of the musical "Oliver!" From just offstage, I peek out at my 12-year-old daughter.

Her hair is tousled, her face is smudged with coal. The dark circles under her eyes are partly makeup, and partly from a tiring four-month rehearsal schedule. She and the other orphans march onto the stage and straight into a dream she has had since she was a tiny kid, always trying to organize other kids on the block to do a play.

I had long wondered how I'd feel at this moment. Pride? Anxiety? Glee? Myocardial infarction?

Standing here, what I mostly feel is grateful. I am grateful that she has found something she is good at – something to increase her confidence and her sense of personal responsibility as she enters the turbulent years of adolescence. And I am grateful that there are institutions like these – community theaters, kids' sports leagues, gymnastics clubs – groups run on a shoestring, mostly, by volunteers who believe there ought to be places where kids can discover themselves.

It was back in October that she saw the audition notice for "Oliver!" She begged to try out this time. She was too young when they did "Annie" and too young for "A Christmas Carol." But now, she said, she was ready.

"You can audition on three conditions," we told her. "First, you have to work really hard to prepare for it, because it will be scary and you have to be ready. Second, you can't be discouraged if you don't get a part, because there will be a lot of talented kids trying. And third, if you do get in, you can't let your grades slip because your school work comes first."

"I promise, I promise, I promise," she said.

We knew Rachel was in a crucial year. She had left the snuggly confines of elementary school. As a sixth-grader in middle school, her workload had tripled. And many of her friends were having identity crises. They were caking on the makeup, going ga-ga over boys, and some were already copping a bad attitude toward school.

Maybe it was counter-intuitive to let our child take on something as big as a musical right now. But we took the gamble. She and her girlfriends are entering a period of uncertainty. Many will feel their own value subordinated. They'll be asked to lead cheers for the boys' teams, to primp for the boys' admiration. The stronger their sense of self, we figured, the better they can deal with adolescence.

She dove into preparing for the audition. I called on an old friend, a professional singer, to coach her. It was astounding how Rachel's singing voice grew. "You're going to knock them out," we assured her on the night before the audition.

We were less certain in the morning. There were 104 kids in the theater, waiting to audition for only 20 kids' parts; 80 of them were girls, trying to get just 10 girls' parts.

"I'm scared," she said.

"You're ready," I answered.

She was No. 48. Kid after talented kid handed sheet music to the pianist and took the stage alone. Some belted it out. Others nearly collapsed. The theater was atremble.

I wanted to tell her that if she just did her best, I'd be the proudest parent there. But all that came out was, "Don't forget to breathe!"

On stage she announced her name in a barely audible voice. Oh no, I thought, she's lost it. But when she heard the opening notes of her song, she drew in a gulp of oxygen and something sparked. Her voice filled the theater.

They called her back that afternoon to dance and act, and that night she made the cast. She wept with joy.

Rehearsals began in December, three nights a week, then four, then five, and finally six nights a week in the last spurt before the show opened for a five-week run. It was grueling. She had little free time; homework filled all her spare minutes. She fought to stay healthy, but the flu got her during the final week. She hung tough.

Through it all, she learned about responsibility. Backstage, she was treated as an adult. Nobody would pick up after her or remind her of what to do. Acting out her childhood fantasy required some growing up.

Her grades went up. She was carrying a 3.46 grade point average before the audition, but during the Oliver rehearsals, it rose to 3.86 – six A's and a B. The more she took on, the more she excelled.

Now the moment arrives. My kid has come face to face with her dream. I suck in my breath and hold it as she and her chums belt out the chorus of "Food, Glorious Food." I don't let it out again until 2½ hours later as they sing the last bars of the finale.

She comes downstage for her bow, and I finally exhale. The play is open! The ovation is huge! They've done it! She's made it! My little girl is growing up …

Suddenly, I gasp. There, in the middle of the stage, completely out of place, are her shoes.

A pair of 1998 beach clogs in the middle of Dickens' London. My daughter's clogs. She had run out to take her bow as a barefoot orphan, but had forgotten that one detail – to take her shoes off. So she had wriggled out of them, right onstage. And now, everyone is dancing around those clogs!

Oh well. At least she's not growing up too fast.

Who Are These People, Stealing Children?

My wife's voice whistled over the phone with a windchill factor of 40 below zero.

"There's been another kidnapping, and this time it's in Placerville," she said, a parent's agony apparent in her tone.

It was closing time on a Wednesday. I'd just called to say hi, that I'd be working late but I'd still get home in time for her to go to Jazzercise.

And she tells me the story that she just saw on TV.

A 13-year-old boy, Shawn Truesdale, is in the grocery store – the grocery store where we shop. He tells his dad he's going to the bathroom. When he comes out, someone grabs him. A man in a plaid shirt. He yanks the boy out the back door and shoves him under the dashboard of a pickup truck.

The boy is crying as he tells the TV crews of his decision to leap from the truck speeding down Highway 50. He figured his chances were better that way.

He survived the jump, a miracle. But now what? What will this boy see when he closes his eyes?

My wife won't be going to Jazzercise tonight. She wants to stay home. Put the girls in the bath. Touch their hair, look at their faces, smile at the things they'll say.

They'll say things like, "Fog is just clouds that have fallen down ripe." Or, when morning light splinters into the bedroom and glints across her face, "Look, momma, sun leaks are playing on you."

They see the world that way, our children. But do we have the right to let them go on seeing just the beauty and delight? How do we train them to be street smart? Do we tell them about these kidnappings? And what will that rob them of? Will they figure out that fog is just fog and light is just light?

Tonight, my wife wants to stay home where it's safe, and right now she never wants any of us to step foot out that front door again.

And as she's telling me this, my heart darkens like the Jack of Spades.

I want to know who these people are, stealing children. Stealing my wife's peace of mind. Stealing my kids' freedom to see fairies while they play in the front yard.

I have taught myself to be a non-violent man, by moral choice, but I want to tear these people to shreds. I am a benevolent man, but I want these thieves to suffer unutterable horrors.

Last summer there was Jaycee Dugard up in Tahoe. Someone grabbed her right off the street. Then there were other reports of attempted kidnappings in Folsom, in Carmichael, in North Highlands, in Diamond Springs, in Stockton. Hysteria? Then in December a 4-year-old child was stolen in Fairfield. Right off the street. In her own neighborhood, where a child should be free to romp.

And now the boy in my neighborhood.

It's hard being a parent. I suppose it always has been. My grandparents had to worry about pneumonia, smallpox. My folks sweated it out over polio.

We conquered those, us humans. The disease we didn't figure on was us.

Sometimes I want to move to some tiny island. Just float off where there aren't any people. Worry about malaria and beriberi. That would be better than worrying about the car coming up the street.

I remember before Kelli and I had the kids, we'd engage in those lengthy nighttime talks with our other childless friends, wondering, all of us, whether it was worth bringing children into this nuclear, polluted, crime-ridden, rat-raced, commercialized, homogenized, impersonalized, dangerous world. "I don't know," we'd shake our heads. "I don't know either."

In our circle of friends, we were the first to have one. It was inadvertence, not fearlessness. And from the moment she began to kick in the womb, all our doubts evaporated.

That's not to say our fears ever left us. Just our doubts. A parent's fears circle like birds of prey.

And sometimes, when I hear my wife's voice go cold and see her bolt the door, I still have my doubts.

I don't want to grow cynical and paranoid, because I don't want to raise cynical, paranoid children. But somehow I've got to give these kids a savvy my generation never needed.

A few weeks ago, Kelli and the kids left the grocery store and stopped for gas just across the street. She noticed the guy standing there, staring at her. She's a woman who lots of men stare at, but this one – she noticed that he smirked as his eyes followed her.

She pulled out onto the street, and his car pulled out behind her. She sped up. He sped up. She turned left. He turned left. Was she imagining this? She whipped into a parking lot. He got hung in traffic, trying to follow. She veered behind a store, then watched him drive past, unable to see her.

She sped home, whisked the children inside, bolted the door. Didn't go to Jazzercise.

Kids are brilliant and wonderful and capable. But they're so damned vulnerable. They belong on tiny islands somewhere. They are tiny islands, in a big stormy sea.

I Know What Those Boys Are Thinking

This afternoon, 18 seventh-graders will descend upon my house for the 13th birthday party of my daughter Rachel.

Half of them will be boys.

In the immortal words of Colonel Kurtz in "Apocalypse Now," the horror, the horror.

I am frantically trying to think of what kinds of activities to make available so that this doesn't devolve into one big makeout party – the kind we used to have when I was in seventh grade.

I've been pumping air into the basketballs and making sure the hoop looks alluring. I have purchased an extra supply of badminton birdies. The old croquet set never looked better.

The hot tub is ... No – wait a minute! I don't want the little bastards in the hot tub.

Does anybody have a pingpong table? A trampoline? A climbing rock? Anything that will absorb energy and cause the testosterone to ricochet in some direction other than toward my daughters and their girlfriends.

Rachel has wanted a boy-girl birthday party since – well, since she was old enough to know the difference, which in her case was on the way home from the maternity ward. She began lobbying heavily last summer. And she is a very effective lobbyist.

Two weeks ago, I caved.

"OK," I said. "But only six boys and six girls."

"Twelve and 12," she countered.

"Eight."

"Eleven."

"Nine then. The boys come at 3 o'clock and leave at 4. The girls can stay till 7."

"How about the boys come at noon and leave at 9, and the girls stay all weekend?"

"You're dreaming. The girls can stay the night, but I want the boys out of here before dark. Before dark."

"OK, but you and mom have to stay upstairs."

"No way! This is going to be supervised, and if you don't like that, I'm going to show up in a clown costume."

That broke her. We settled at nine boys, nine girls; boys here from 2 till 6; girls stay for a slumber party; adult supervision; lots of activities.

"And no making out," I snarled.

She was too embarrassed to answer.

We have always tried to have a very open rapport with our kids. My wife and I don't shy away from any subject. Our only rule is that there are no secrets in our family.

But now, the days we've been preparing them for are near at hand. And I'm thinking we should have sent them to a nunnery.

"How are we going to keep them out of the woods?" my wife asks.

Our house is surrounded by about 500 acres. The girls have been out there hiking like Davy Crockett and Daniel Boone since we moved in three months ago. The trails through the forest are one of the things they want to show off to their friends.

A wave of panic. How are we going to keep them out of the woods? My shoulders sag. For a moment, resignation descends on me.

"Maybe we shouldn't even try," I say. "Maybe we should just accept the fact that this is all part of growing up."

"Right," my wife wisecracks. "And you could give the boys a little speech when they arrive about how to use a condom."

That jars me out of my defeatism.

"Oh, I'll show 'em how to use a condom all right," I say in my best George Patton growl. "Get me some of those Playtex rubber gloves. They can use those as condoms. The little bastards."

We settle on a strategy of four hours of intense activities. Rachel suggests they might want to dance – I think that's what she means by "jam" – so I string up some speakers by the patio and have her select a pile of CDs with really fast, heavy rock 'n' roll that you couldn't slow-dance to if you were freezing to death in a blizzard.

Forlorn, waiting for the young barbarians to arrive, I sit by the window in the family room and watch the clock. The hour hand is going way too fast. So, for that matter, are the pages on the calendar.

There's a photo album on the bookshelf next to me. It opens to a picture of Rachel on the old sofa, 2 years old, giving a big kiss to her baby sister, Lauren.

Just outside the window, my girls – now 13 and 11 – are setting up the croquet set. I look back and forth from them to the picture. Their baby fat is gone. They are slender, graceful from growing up in dance shoes. But they still shine the way they did when they were tiny.

I couldn't see it so much when they were babies, but now their family resemblances peek out with every new shard of light that glints upon them. They turn this way and I see an aunt, that way and I see a grandmother. Mostly, they are lucky enough to look like their mother – and not like me. No, somehow they don't look like me.

My reverie is broken by a knock at the door.

There stand a couple of the boys, shifting awkwardly on their feet, looking at the ground, avoiding my eyes, mumbling.

And it hits me.

They look like me. Exactly like me – back when I was their age.

And I know exactly what's in their filthy little minds.

The little bastards.

A Tribute to Those Who Come and Go

Rachel burst from the womb into the world with her eyes wide open.

Far away, jet fighters careened over North Africa, Halley's Comet streaked through the cosmos and a volcano erupted in the Aleutians.

In another wing of the hospital that same night, even as my astounded little daughter was getting her first, gasping glimpse of the planet, a friend was getting her last.

Lessie Goodrich was one of those people so full of life, it is difficult now, two months later, to conceive of her being gone so suddenly. But a massive stroke felled her and she didn't have a chance to meet baby Rachel, the latest in a line of many children Lessie cared about.

Lessie died within hours of Rachel's birth.

She was a walker, Lessie – a real walker. Every afternoon in every season, year in and year out, she went sauntering on the hilly streets of Placerville. She took long, hurtling steps with the swift pace of a curious person, one who is dedicated to taking everything in.

I close my eyes and can still see Lessie walking past on the sidewalk. I recall her boisterous voice and the smile she always flashed so generously.

Rachel wants to go for a stroll, so I gather her up in my arms and we walk into the twilight of a brilliant spring day.

Her eyes are as blue as the river we walk beside and as wide open as the sky above. She struggles to take everything in. She is a curious child, this Rachel. It will be months before she takes her first steps, but already I fancy Rachel will be a walker, too.

By another striking coincidence, Rachel's birthday was on the third anniversary of my grandfather's death in the same hospital. This uncanny balance of birth and death, and the seemingly interwoven threads that draw our lives together, baffle me and make me spin off on that endless search for the lessons we primates are so fond of.

It is seldom that one gets such a profound sense of the fleeting nature of life. Looking into my daughter's eyes, I am overwhelmed by how short our time is.

As we walk by the river, I think of the places I've been – places I seldom go anymore. The demands of a career, the promise of a family, the restrictions of growing needs, have suddenly cast upon me a heavy crown of responsibility. I can't find the time that had seemed so abundant through the better part of 32 roving years.

And yet there is no remorse, for in this child is renewal. Looking into her face affirms that there is a reason for all of this toil and trouble. It melts the cynicism right out of me. I find an infinite surge of optimism there in Rachel's eyes.

They grow heavy-lidded and we head for home.

We're in another baby boom, I hear. Everybody's doing it. Yuppies are breeding like guppies. Babies are chic little units.

It will be intriguing to watch a generation that gave its own parents such a hard time step into that demanding role. Parenting is an art that goes far beyond learning to sleep when the baby isn't looking, and I have yet to be convinced mine is a generation of any greater artistry than generations past.

Child rearing is paradoxical in essence: We seek to give our children roots while at the same time we attempt to give them wings.

It's one of the most intimidating jobs you can do, and yet one of the simplest. It doesn't matter how deliberately you plot strategies about the values you will teach your children. Your truths and your lies will be there, written on the clean slate of your child's nature, no matter what you plan. The most you can do is to try to be honest about which of your qualities are good, which are bad, and then watch them as they appear.

"If you must hold yourself up to your children as an object lesson," wrote George Bernard Shaw, "hold yourself up as a warning and not as an example."

I want Rachel to be curious, a wide-eyed walker like Lessie, taking it all in with a certain savvy and a bouncy stride.

But more, I want her to inherit my grandfather's compassion and tolerance.

I don't mind her being skeptical, but I hope she grows up free of the cynicism that blinds so many of us as we age. Life is limitless for the person who looks on the world with the untainted eye of a child.

Most of all, I want Rachel to have the courage to be a dreamer.

As I lay her down in her white bassinet – the antique bassinet that our friend Lessie loaned us – my daughter stirs softly . . . and then sleeps.

I sense that Rachel is dreaming, and I envy her the sweet ones.

Far away, a comet speeds off into the universe, and a volcano ceases to rumble.

Having Holidays at the Holidays is Bad Timing

'Twas the last week or two before Christmas, and all through my house, tension was building, and I was a louse.

A pattern seems to be developing around my place. Every year, my wife and I work so hard to create a Norman Rockwell sort of holiday season that we wind up too tired and tense to enjoy what we've worked to create.

We're so American. We want it all.

We want The Traditional Christmas. A well-trimmed tree, wreaths of holly, halls decked with mistletoe. Sleighbells jingling, Bing Crosby crooning, Santa grinning. Family and friends with whom to share it.

We want The Christmas of Presents and Gifts – not because we're greedy and indulgent, necessarily, but because we want to give each other symbols of how we feel.

We want The Christmas of Generosity to those less fortunate. Donating time to the food bank, the hospital, collecting gifts for the needy. These have become important to us.

We want The Spiritual Christmas. At some point we need to meditate on the life of that baby in the manger, or else be left with a feeling of emptiness.

Above all, we want The Warmth of Having Christmas Together. We want our little family to renew its strength.

Through the years we've found that if any of these elements is missing, the holidays get out of kilter. Christmas doesn't seem whole.

But it's an awful lot for a family to accomplish. It requires careful planning and hard work. And it comes right in the middle of flu season.

For each goal there are obstacles.

The Traditional Christmas means slogging through the forest in a hunt for the right tree. It means a car full of pine needles. Digging the patented Wobbly Tree Stand out of the attic. Untangling the lights. Pine pitch on my hands. A decade's worth of ornaments for my wife to sort through. Stringing lights on an icy roof. Eggnog spilled on the carpet by amped-up kids. Cats and dogs demolishing carefully arranged manger scenes. Putting on a feast for my side of the family, then quickly regrouping to attend a feast with her side of the family.

The Christmas of Presents and Gifts means we must choose between spending more money than we ought to, or less than we would like to. Either way, it takes effort to look for the right gifts. We must try to convince kids that the stuff they see on TV isn't worth wishing for – that they'd really prefer an educational computer program. Then we buy the toys anyway. And then there are the little gifts we want to give friends and relatives; it will mean more if we make them ourselves.

The Christmas of Generosity means an investment of time, energy and money. Buy and wrap gifts, put together some food baskets. My wife makes cookies for the baskets – dozens and dozens of cookies. She organizes activities for kids – our kids and lots of other peoples' kids, at school and through Girl Scouts. I too give time to organizations – and time is hard to come by this time of the year.

The Spiritual Christmas. Somewhere in the mix it would be nice to attend a midnight mass. Somewhere in the mix. Around midnight.

So when, exactly, are we going to feel The Warmth of Having Christmas Together? Maybe it'll come when we decorate the tree? Nope – I get tense when the tree falls over. Maybe it'll come when we bake cookies? Nope – my wife gets upset because the kids wanted to do this and now they won't help. Maybe it'll come when we have the relatives over for a feast? Nope – somebody complains about the food we worked two days to prepare.

Sometimes it feels as if we've been sold a load of goods. The joys of Christmas have been marketed so heavily to us all our lives that they've now become unattainable. We're left feeling frustrated and inadequate that we can't make our Christmas look like the ad campaigns.

Bit by bit, piece by piece, we've tried to simplify things. We've tried to jettison that which doesn't work.

We've curtailed the gift thing. Last year, we worked out a gift exchange with my side of the family where we each draw a name to buy for, and then we focus on finding something special for that one person. This year, my wife and I set a pretty tight budget for our gifts to each other, and we may even stick to it. And we're shopping now from catalogs instead of in malls.

Of course, the time and money we've saved seems to have been absorbed by things we're doing with community organizations. But it's a definite improvement.

We selected a tree in record time this year – spurred along by the pouring rain.

Of course, I caught the flu.

Our most radical departure was made a month ago when we decided not to host the Christmas Eve feast.

My wife and I were at a weekend conference near Yosemite. The valley was so beautiful, uncrowded and covered with snow. We looked at each other and said, hey, why don't we come here for Christmas? Before the impulse could pass, we reserved a room for the three days leading up to Christmas, using actual cash.

Of course, then came the part where I had to tell my family that we weren't going to have everyone over for Christmas Eve dinner this year.

Now my sister's mad at me. She says Christmas traditions don't mean enough to anyone anymore.

Maybe she's right. At least, the Christmas tradition that we've started to develop at my house doesn't mean much to me – the tradition of feeling stressed out because not everything is living up to tradition.

Next year, I think we'll celebrate Christmas in July – when not so much is going on.

Birthday Planning is One of Life's Hurdles

Birthdays at my house have become something of an endurance test. First up every year is my wife's birthday in March. She's relatively easy to please. That's exactly what makes it so difficult to plan for her birthday.

It's very intimidating, for example, to shop for a present for a person who is easy to please, because you have an unlimited universe of items from which to choose. Worse still, with my wife, you're shopping for an extremely experienced shopper. Anything you get her, she's going to be thinking in the back of her head, "I saw a better one at that little store in Auburn," or, "I hope he didn't pay too much for this – they have it at Target for $3.99."

She doesn't want you to throw her a party. Veiled behind her shrugging persona, however, is the subtle message that you'd better plan something. Make it something romantic. Sweet. Kind. Clever. Ingenious. Sensitive.

A party would be easier.

Just a week after I have survived my wife's birthday comes my eldest daughter's birthday. Unlike my wife, my eldest daughter is not easy to please.

Theoretically, considering the case of my wife – who is easy to please and therefore difficult to please – it should be easy to please my eldest daughter, who is not easy to please.

Unfortunately, it's not that simple. Under the Quantum Law of Inverse and Corresponding Birthday Expectations, she is even more difficult to please, because everything done for her must top everything that was done one week earlier for my wife.

Gifts are not the issue with Rachel. With her, what counts is the party you throw. She's a social little critter and she loves a good party. Therefore, she knows a good party from a bad one.

A few years back, we made the mistake of throwing Rachel a theme birthday party – a Wizard of Oz birthday party. I found myself decorating the entire house as Kansas and turning the back yard into a colorful Oz, complete with yellow bricks. The following year, of course, we tried to top that. And last year, things got out of hand with a dress-up party. Her bedroom was turned into a boutique full of used clothes. As her friends arrived, they were first escorted into the boutique, where my wife helped them select a wardrobe, and all the aunts applied make-up. They were then shown to an elaborate table on the back deck, where I stood in a black tuxedo, hair slicked back, playing the role of François the French waiter.

Out of hand, I'm telling ya.

Next comes my birthday in May, and the splendor of spring is overshadowed by my dark and gloomy mood.

I almost turned 40 last year – 38, in fact, a close call – and I behaved so miserably that my entire family hated me. Suffice it to say that my wife now insists that if I ever really do turn 40, 1 travel to Montana. Alone.

Last and most challenging of all comes my youngest daughter's birthday.

Lauren, our second child, was born on Dec. 20, 1987. She is in a category all her own – easy to please and not easy to please. Laws of the birthday universe do not apply to her. With Lauren, we face not one, not even two, but three serious birthday minefields.

First, there's the issue of gifts. Like her mom, Lauren is a consummate shopper, honing her skills on the zillions of TV commercials she sees while her sister is off at school.

Second, like her sister, Lauren is a social little critter. She knows a good theme party when she sees one. And by gosh, her party better be at least as good as Rachel's.

And third, guarding against second-child syndrome, we don't want Lauren to experience the feelings of unworthiness that she surely would have if we had her party five days before Christmas and people were allowed to double up on her presents. So we throw Lauren a birthday party late in November. The celebration, however, tends to last until New Year's.

And so last Saturday morning dawned to find me rummaging through garbage bins all over town, looking for huge cardboard boxes that once held refrigerators.

Lauren, you see, had decided that her birthday party this year would have a tropical theme – a luau.

After collecting big cardboard boxes and nearly being bit by a massive black widow spider, I started cutting out cardboard palm trees. My wife and Rachel painted them with tempera on the front lawn while Lauren presided. Then we cut out pineapples. And coconuts. Then we went to the crafts store. We had to buy plastic flowers for leis, because real flowers are hard to find in November. And then we had to figure out a way to make grass skirts, because nobody sells grass skirts in November, and who ever heard of a luau in November anyway? And then I had to hit the record stores looking for slack-key Hawaiian guitar music, which ain't easy to find.

I'm drawing the line at roast pig in a pit, knowing full well it could result in paying for Lauren's therapy later.

When the delirium of putting on a luau gets to be too much, I remind myself that we talked Lauren into a luau as a way to persuade her not to demand a Little Mermaid party in which the entire house would have been turned into an aquarium.

Now, if all this sounds as if my children are spoiled . . . They are. We work hard at it. We're good at it.

I guess it's easier to invest in making their birthdays fun now, while they're young, than it would be to let them grow up hating birthdays and having to pay therapists.

Or paying to send them to Montana.

Selling a House is Like Selling a Soul

My face pokes up through the rose vines and is immediately drenched by a driving rain. I should be indoors, sipping hot toddies by the fire. But these rain gutters must be cleaned.

We've decided to sell the house and the Realtor tour is tomorrow.

Yanking out clumps of pine needles and oak leaves, I scan the roof. It has held up well over 12 years. My family has been safe and dry through howling storms.

Ah, there on the roof is the wayward boomerang. It flew splendidly last summer when my kids threw it, but it never seemed to come back like they expected.

I see that the window screen is torn on my 12-year-old's upstairs bedroom. Just a few weeks ago I caught her climbing out of that window to the roof. I have no idea what she was doing. Neither did she. Maybe she was after adventure, or maybe she was driven by the wild call of adolescence. Lately, she's been something of a wayward boomerang herself.

I clean the gutters, prune the roses and move on to the garage.

It won't be easy moving away from this house. So much has happened here, and we've put so much work into the place.

Here's the box of instructions for all the stuff we bought — dishwashers and cameras, windows and wood stoves, pool sweeps and bike pumps, ovens and chop saws, weed whackers and swing sets.

There are instructions here for stuff we don't even have anymore. We need a bigger house just to hold the instructions for all our stuff.

I could leave most of this stuff in the blink of an eye. It has no hold on me. But the house itself – it has as many memories as it has nails.

I find a box of photos. The Realtor wants us to put together a poster, showing what the house looks like when the gardens are in bloom.

Here's a picture of the house when we first bought it. Brand new, the third house in the neighborhood. I'm putting in the sprinklers, ditch-digging with a pickax. There's no lawn, no fence, no gardens, no porch, no decks, no pathways, no climbing roses, no foxgloves, no bricks, no playhouse, no pool.

In this one, Kelli is holding Rachel, who was 6 months old when we came here. My wife had just cropped her hair short, the way new mothers do. Why? Are they so overwhelmed by their new responsibilities that any bit of simplicity is a blessing? Or maybe it's biological. Are they shearing off their mating plumage?

Not enough, I suppose, because little more than a year later, we were expecting again. The second pregnancy was complicated. Kelli had to lay down flat for six months, not even sitting up to eat. It was the most gallant thing I've ever seen anybody do. The joy that filled this house – the entire neighborhood – when we finally had Lauren …

What about that joy? When we sell this house, will we be paid anything for the joy in these walls? How about the sorrows? Will there be a value placed on them?

Here's the place where we buried Rasta the cat, and my kids grieved for the first time. In there, the carpet is worn where they learned to walk.

Everywhere I look, I see our lives.

We almost moved once before, early in 1990 during a real estate boom. Kelli had fallen in love with an old Victorian – right up until the sellers disclosed that the house was haunted by a ghost.

Looking back, I guess that ghost saved us. Soon the California real estate market crashed. It would have taken us right up until about now for that Victorian's value to bounce back to what we would have paid for it.

Now we have found the right house – a friend's house, actually, on 5 acres where it will be easier to keep the world at bay. We almost bought it last summer, but the price was too high for us. So our friends put it on the market and, when no offers came in, they realized that they had put too much value on the sentiments that were in their walls.

A couple of weeks ago, they lowered the price, just as we were deciding that we wanted it after all.

And so here we are, scurrying to sell our home. This place that should be sold in spring, when it is in bloom, will be put on the market in the dead of winter.

Who will make this their home? Will they see the craftsmanship that I tried to bring into each thing I built? Or will they think it's all weird and useless? "Oh God, Henry, those hand-carved turnposts have got to go."

It won't be easy leaving. But there is so much to do before the Realtors descend for the open house tomorrow. I don't have time to digest the lumps in my throat.

We work into the night and then sleep uneasily. My daughters lie in their beds and stare at the familiar patterns in the ceiling – the man in the moon, the frog prince, the ballerina. The patterns look different to them now, viewed through a kaleidoscope of tears.

Morning comes and I'm scurrying around. A dab of touch-up paint here, a pot of snapdragons there.

A knock comes on the door. The real estate agents are here. It's time to make way.

Getting Wisdom Getting Rid of Stuff

Sitting wearily here in my new house, I look around. A forest of boxes is stacked up to the ceiling, with little pygmy trails running through from room to room.

Moving my household has taught me two things. They are not very profound things, I'll admit, but I learned them very profoundly – learned them deeply, you might say, the way you learn there is a splinter under your thumbnail, as there is under mine.

The two things I learned are these:

(1) Moving your household when you are middle-aged is a lot tougher than moving when you were young, because nowadays, all your friends have bad backs.

And (2) we have way too much crap.

I was too cheap to shell out the $1,000 for a professional moving company to come over, scoop up all our stuff and move my family a mile or two from the old house to the new house. So I opted to do it myself.

Stupid, yes, I know that now. But I had visions of moving the way it used to be, before I had two kids and we had spent 12 years in one location, accumulating things.

The last time we moved, when my elder daughter was 6 months

old, we rented a U-Haul truck. Three or four friends showed up in the morning. For the cost of chicken wings and a six-pack of beer, they gave us a hand. We scooped up all the stuff and simply moved it. No big deal. It was finished by dinner.

This time around, it took me 11 days.

You begin to get the sense that it's going to be different a few weeks before the move. Word gets around. Friends begin to avoid you. Others sidle up cautiously.

"I'm there for you," they say, "just as long as it doesn't involve any lifting."

You scratch your head, trying to think of what kind of help you might need during a move that would not involve any lifting. And you schedule a week off work, figuring you're on your own.

Moving day snuck up quickly. In December, faithful readers might recall, my family decided on the spur of a moment to buy a friend's house. We were terribly worried that our old house would not sell and we would go bankrupt. Instead, it was only on the market for one day before we sold it. That left us planning a move with very few days to get organized.

While my wife and kids started boxing things up, I went to the new house, which was empty, and built a great mass of garage shelves. I figured that would make the move easier, because all the stuff from our old garage and attic could just be slipped into the new shelves.

I vastly underestimated the amount of crap we have.

Kelli came down from the attic shaking her head ominously. "There's a lot of crap up there."

We have saved stuff as if there's going to be a museum some day, devoted exclusively to us.

Box after back-breaking box kept tumbling out of the attic: Every Halloween costume the kids ever wore. Broken lamps. Dead cameras. Crates of old record albums, including three copies of "Déjà Vu." My grandfather's smashed fishing pole and a 10-year-old jar of salmon eggs. A collection of salt and pepper shakers. Three tents and a rusty lantern. Every piece of schoolwork the children ever did. Two wobbly rocking chairs and a trombone. Posters from college. Trophies and plaques. Old clothes. Old dishes. Yearbooks. A baby crib. Knickknacks enough for the Smithsonian. Crates of old record albums, including three copies of "Déjá Vu."

What is all this?

A similar torrent of useless stuff seemed to have been stored up in the house itself. We had packed every cupboard and shelf, like people living on a boat.

In no time, the garage shelves at the new house were overflowing.

I rented the U-Haul and my brawny nephew showed up on Day Three to help move the furniture, including a huge wardrobe cabinet that had to go upstairs. He saved my life, that boy.

But after hauling the furniture, there was still an amazing amount of stuff back at the old house. Soon, there was no place to put stuff at the new house.

For eight more days, my wife and I kept moving stuff, pickup truck load by pickup truck load. It just kept coming. In the new house, canyons of boxes piled up.

That's when I started going to the dump.

Taking a load of crap to the dump, I soon realized, was intensely satisfying. Box after box, thrown over the precipice. Flushed into the void. A profound catharsis.

And so it went, on and on, until on the 10th day, my back went out.

Now, sitting here among the boxes and pygmy trails, my lower back hurts so badly that I can't tie my shoe. It takes strategic planning to put on pants. I would like to take a sip of that beer over there, but I cannot reach it.

One of the kids approaches. "Daddy," she says, "can you help me set up my bookshelf?"

"I'm there for you, sweetheart," I say, "just as long as it doesn't involve any lifting."

Falling Apart:
the Diary of a Home
Improvement Project

On a sweltering day last August, we sort of decided we needed a swimming pool. Heat can twist your thinking.

From August to October we work on our rationale. It's no longer convenient just to traipse off to a river to swim. It'll give the kids something to do at home, since the neighborhoods aren't safe anymore. And when the kids are teenagers, their friends will want to hang out at our pool instead of some opium den across town.

And besides, Wifey wants one. The Process begins.

October: We get bids from five contractors. "Pool contractors are notorious flakes, you know," a friend warns me. But they aren't flaky about bidding. They show up for sales pitches right on time. I have very little idea what they're talking about but the drawings are pretty.

November: To pay for this, we start to refinance, playing the waiting game to lock in at just the right moment. In late November when we finally lock in, the interest rates have jogged up half a point from where they had been in August. A month later they'll be back down. Too bad.

Wifey experiences first dizzy spells.

Dec. 15: We sign contract to have prettiest picture built. Last full night of sleep.

Jan. 2: Before the pool job can begin, cedar tree must be removed. I get a frantic call at work. "My God, what have we done?" Wifey says. "They're taking down the tree!" Condescendingly, I reassure her, "Gee, you wanted a pool. This will make our life better, remember?"

Later, I come home. The whole neighborhood smells like cedar. I think I hear the tree's ghost moaning.

At 2 am., we're both wide awake. "My God, what have we done?" we ask each other over and over until dawn, while the cedar ghost whimpers outside.

Jan. 3: Household stress is building. Wifey's dizzy spells evolve to migraine. Daughter No. 2 develops flu, tonsillitis, bronchitis and sinus infection, all at once.

Jan. 5-8: Tree service fails to show up to grind cedar stump. I lay bricks to finish a planter, dig ditches to reroute sprinklers, build a small retaining wall, chop wood.

At midnight I wake up. Pain is shooting through my rib cage. "A heart attack," I think "That's it. This is The Big One!" I lay there for 45 minutes, hyperventilating in a pool of sweat. Then I realize it's a pulled muscle.

Jan. 9: Tree service grinds stump and prized azalea.

Meanwhile, I'm building retaining wall, laying bricks, ruining back. Wifey still having dizzy spells. Daughter No. 2 sick as a dog. Dog pees in house for first time ever.

Jan. 17: Big burly excavator and two scrawny henchmen show up to dig pool. Burly growls and scowls a lot. "No pictures," he snarls at Wifey. Later, he hints at bankruptcy and alimony problems.

Designer shows up to help lay out pool. Wifey says she wants to make changes. Burly excavator's face turns purple. I shrink in corner. She gets migraine.

Digging begins. Burly excavator's personality changes. He begins to beam. He's like a sculptor at work, wheeling his Bobcat tractor around in tight spaces, pulling out 22 truckloads of dirt. I praise him. "It's like part of my body," he beams, patting the Bobcat.

Then he stops smiling. "We hit a shelf of rock," he says. An expensive gizmo will have to be rented if he can't jackhammer the rock out tomorrow. The henchmen look perturbed. They'll be running the jackhammer.

Jan. 18: Excavator returns. Jackhammer cranks up. The job is done by noon. No fancy gizmo to rent. So far so good.

Wifey and Daughter No. 2 go to doctor. I begin to repair damage to front yard from Bobcat, including mined sprinkler system. Rare lilac is a goner.

Jan. 19: Electrician, plumber and rebar guys all show up on time. By end of the day the pool is plumbed, wired and ready for concrete. This is unbelievable.

Jan. 21: Gunnite crew shows up on time. Wifey says they're far cuter than excavation and plumbing crew. Her health improves. Concrete sprayed in just as rain begins.

Jan. 22: It's pouring. I still have work to do, putting sprinklers in trenches and moving dirt that has now turned into mud. I work in downpour, slogging about in a back yard so trenched up it looks like the battlefield at Gallipoli. I lose a Wellington boot in the mud. Pool seems ridiculous.

Tension running high, Wifey begins to have severe stomach cramps and intestinal unrest. Daughter No. 1 develops rash on hand that quickly spreads to entire body making her look like a strawberry. Antibiotics have cured Daughter No. 2 but she announces she wants to quit ballet lessons.

Jan. 28: After many days of rain, tile guy shows up, sets tile. Looks good.

Jan. 29, 30: We spend weekend carefully preparing area around pool to be landscaped and putting drainage ditch in front yard, until Wifey's stomach cramps up. Daughter No. 1's rash is massive, undiagnosed, and she wants to quit piano lessons. Daughter No. 2 throws four tantrums. Dog pees in bathtub.

Jan. 31: Brick man shows up to build decking. Arrogant guy. Promptly insults Wifey, then proceeds to pile dirt on and generally bash all areas we had prepared for landscaping. Works three hours to undo our weekend efforts, then leaves. Wifey schedules fourth doctor visit of month.

Feb. 1: I meet with brick man. Arrogant guy. Promptly insults all my brickwork. Changes plans for decking. Informs me I can't have bullnosed coping I wanted. Manages to jack up price of job anyway.

Then leaves.

Feb. 2: Brick guy puts coping around pool. Says he'll return tomorrow to pour cement foundation.

Feb. 3: Wifey accidentally turns on sprinkler system. Broken pipes cause massive flooding. My new drainage ditches don't drain. Brick guy shows up, assesses damages, insults ditches, goes home. Wifey begins to develop a tumor.

Feb. 4: Brick guy pours cement pad. Trashes all remaining living landscape in process.

Daughter No. 1's rash is beginning to clear, but both daughters now want to quit Girl Scouts.

Feb. 5: Brick guy doesn't show. Wifey has Metamucil delivered in bulk. If she doesn't need it all, we'll use what's left as soil conditioner.

Feb. 6, 7: Still no brick guy. General contractor argues with Wifey over who pays $40 to fix design flaw. Our first spat. Wifey schedules appointment with surgeon.

Feb. 8: Brick guy shows. Lays some bricks. Splashes mortar on redwood deck. Wifey gets on phone and schedules appointment for second opinion, unhappy that the first surgeon suggested she participate in medical experiment involving placebos.

Late in evening, unable to sleep, I pull out pool contract for light reading. Am amazed to see that every single thing that has come up to piss me off since this project began is covered by the contract. Pool contractor isn't liable for any of it.

Guess I should have read the contract more carefully. Rash appears on my finger. Daughter No. 2 has the flu.

Feb. 9-17: Brick guy lays bricks on days when weather is clear. Grumbles steadily about having to make hundreds of cuts. Most of his work is beautiful, I must admit, until the last day, when he builds a step that sags severely in the middle due to the weight of his attitude.

Feb. 19: I am injured in a shoveling accident. Happens while digging deep drainage trench on a rainy day with a two-handled post-hole digger. In ramming the digger down into a trench next to a retaining wall, a bolt on the digger hangs up against wall. With all my weight I ram my eyesockets down on top of the handles – a perfect fit, one eyesocket per handle. I sit in the mud for half an hour, dazed, trying to remember the capital of Zimbabwe.

Feb. 22-27: Just two steps left before the pool is done. Electrician must show up and install pool equipment and then plaster guy must show up and plaster. Weather is perfect for both jobs. Neither guy shows.

I take opportunity to read up on pool maintenance. Realize I should never have cheated to pass chemistry. Using year 2000 dollars, I start to project the costs of removing a slimy concrete pond from a back yard, but soon lapse into fitful sleep.

Daughter No. 2 has rash on her bottom. Whole family's throats are sore.

Feb. 29: Equipment installed. In a related incident, gas water heater stops working.

Mar. 1: Day begins with cold shower. I run naked into living room, trying to get warm, only to find crew of plasterers outside living room window staring in.

Day ends with water filling finished pool. Wifey calls from poolside. "I'm sitting in my lounge chair, having a soda next to my new pool," she boasts. "It's beautiful.

"I'm starting to feel much better," she adds.

Mar. 2: I'm sitting poolside, staring at landscaping to be done, chemicals I must master, mortgage, energy and medical bills I must pay. Heart begins to palpitate.

The Hazards of Home Ownership, Part 2

The rain came, the air went cold and the season changed suddenly. It always changes suddenly when I'm building something around the house. Always for the worse.

If I'm moving tons of dirt with my bare hands to make a new garden terrace, it will suddenly become hotter than camel gas in the Sahara. If I'm laying bricks, the fog will move in overnight so that working on my knees is akin to hard labor in a London debtor's prison circa 1850.

Or like two weeks ago, if I'm completing a 400-square-foot redwood deck that could really use a quick coat of deck oil in order to protect my $1,200 investment, it will rain. Leaves and pine needles will stick all over the redwood, each one leaving a little stain that must be sanded off. And when I get down on my knees to start sanding, it'll turn 100 degrees. Until I get ready to stain. Then it'll rain again.

Such are the perils they don't tell you about in those Sunset and Ortho do-it-yourself books — you know, the ones with women in aprons constructing massive rock walls.

When I bought a new house five years ago, I gazed proudly at my little lot. Mine, all mine. I pounded my chest, yodeled like Tarzan and set about coming up with a plan to civilize the place. The lot was all bare dirt and steep, useless angles. Like the Dutch battling the North Sea for every inch of ground, I would make full use of this land.

Let's see. It would need a lawn and an automatic sprinkler system.

A fence and a few gates. A roof over the back porch. A retaining wall to level off this slope. A deck over that slope. Some brick planters – I'll build fountains into them. And the kids could use a playhouse.

No problem. I'll put in the sprinkler system this weekend.

It was September 1986. 1 remember that because of how hard the ground is in September. I tried to dig several hundred feet of trenches for the sprinklers, by hand, in a country that was made famous by hard-rock mining.

Three or four weekends later, the sprinklers were in and a sod lawn covered them. That wasn't so bad, I thought, mopping my brow with blistered fingers. Now I'll build about 200 feet of fence and get started on the retaining wall.

I took a week off work, expecting to have the fence up by mid-week and then to start the retaining wall.

By the end of my one-week vacation, I had erected only about 12 feet of fence. I also made the grim discovery that post holes can be even tougher to dig than trenches. I rented a one-man gas-powered posthole digger that nearly threw me to Nevada every time I hit a rock, but still spent the better part of three days just digging holes.

Two years later, when about half of the fence was done, I got started on the big retaining wall – the one I originally thought I would start after finishing the fence during that one-week vacation. It would be 30 feet long, 4 feet high and would require backfilling an area about 8 feet wide.

I built the wall by myself, using fancy and extremely expensive interlocking concrete blocks. I backfilled it with 38 truckloads of dirt and gravel, one truckload at a time, over the course of nearly a year. Since I don't have a pickup, I had to borrow trucks and trailers from friends and relatives. They came to hate me, but that's just one of the things those do-it-yourself books forget to tell you – people will start hating you for borrowing their tools and trucks.

The highlight of the retaining wall vigil came when my wife's cousin and I used his utility trailer to find out that dirt you get for free at a construction site is sometimes a lot heavier than dirt you buy at a landscape supplier. We saw some guy with a backhoe and had him fill the trailer. The trailer began to whipsaw down the highway when we were going about 50 mph, casting us wildly from one lane to another until finally flipping over and breaking its hitch and safety chain. That left us in the rather embarrassing predicament of sitting beside the road, our lives still flashing before our eyes, and wondering what to do about 2 tons of dirt and an abused trailer that we had just deposited in the slow lane.

Like I said, there are things the books don't bring up.

Next I figured it was a good idea to start putting a roof over the back porch. This time I got smart and employed the help of a neighbor well-versed in such efforts. We actually covered the porch in just a couple of weeks. It was relatively plumb and level, and even somewhat pleasant looking. Of course, when we put a hot tar roof on, it rained. Now the porch leaks like a sieve. But it's shady.

I learned bricklaying, and in building my flower beds became a firm proponent of never ever using straight lines in garden design. Of course, I had intended to build straight flower beds, until bricklaying began. In the fog, it is difficult to discern that you have veered far off your original course.

I built a couple of garden terraces out of huge 2-by-14-inch redwood boards. Nobody wanted to let me borrow his truck or trailer to go to the lumberyard for the boards, so I shoved them inside my wife's 4Runner. First time I hit a bump, the boards teeter-tottered and broke the windshield.

Last summer's labors produced for my children the Taj Mahal of playhouses. Built to exceed earthquake codes in Mongolia. I dumped $1,000 and demolished three of my favorite fingernails in the process. It's a cute little Victorian.

My kids never play in it. They want a tree house instead. Maybe someday they'll use the playhouse for having premarital sex. For now, it's vacant.

And then, of course, came the deck. My greatest achievement, largely because of the help of a skilled friend. And it's already rotting because I can't get the deck oil down.

So far, I figure I've spent roughly $12,175 on what my wife likes to call "little projects." I have no idea what I've spent on tools. And medical bills. And towing charges for flipped utility trailers. And playhouse-sized condom dispensers.

I am within sight of taming my land, of being done with all this work, of being able to relax and enjoy my place.

Guess it's about time to move to a bigger place.

Yellow Jackets Take Over the World

Humanoids are under siege. It's the yellow jackets. Never in my life have I seen so many freaking yellow jackets.

Mind you, I do not dislike them. I appreciate their role in the environment. I try not to harm them.

But they are beginning to bug me.

The other day I came home, stepped gingerly around some wasps who were partying on a sprinkler head, and found my wife on the couch with her foot propped up on a pillow. One of her toes had swelled up like a plum.

"A yellow jacket got me," she said in a little-girl voice.

Oh great, I thought. She's going to milk this. I'll be preparing dinner all week.

"What do you want for dinner?" I asked.

"Do you mean tonight, or tomorrow?"

My youngest daughter, Lauren, still milks a now-legendary attack at Girl Scout camp three years ago. Her troop was doing an exercise called "hug-a-tree." Lauren hugged a tree with a wasp nest in it.

After about 20 searing stings, my little daughter – whom I had carefully taught to respect and never fear bees – called me from the emergency room.

"Daddy, I hugged the wrong tree," she sobbed. "The yellow jackets got me."

"That's what I heard, honey. I wish I was there with you."

"Daddy? Can you stop on the way home and buy me a doll?"

Three years later, I'm still paying off things she's coaxed me to buy as salve for the trauma of hugging the wrong tree.

On the bright side, I guess all these yellow jackets are creating a positive economic ripple. Last weekend, I went to six stores shopping for yellow-jacket traps. The shelves were bare.

This is a bumper year, according to news reports. Twenty-one kids were stung in an Oakland park last week. A Wisconsin man slammed his minivan into a tree and perished after yellow jackets swarmed him.

With such reports buzzing in my head, and yellow jackets swarming in the yard, and dishes piling up in the sink, I decided on Saturday to get out of Dodge. "C'mon kids," said I, "we're going to the river."

Within minutes of finding a perfect spot on the South Fork, my body had become a tourist Mecca for hornets, yellow jackets and meat bees of every stripe.

Stay cool, I told myself. These creatures flitting about you serve an important purpose. They kill flies and many destructive insects. Their scavenging helps animal waste to decompose. They are all God's Creatures.

"Goddamnit!" I hollered, flailing my arms like a Pentecostal minister, "get away, you little bastards!"

Back at home, I scrounged in my garage for anything suitably murderous to flying insects. I found a spray can, half full. Armed, I went hunting for their nest.

It didn't take long. Under the eaves, above the front door, there it was – a nest crawling with yellow jackets as big as peanuts.

I lifted the can, shut one eye and aimed – but was saved by the realization that those buzzards were going to make mincemeat out of me if I pulled the trigger.

Ever so slowly, I lowered the can and backed into the house. "Tonight," I muttered, "we'll see who's boss."

I barbecued some chicken and managed to pry enough loose from the yellow jackets to feed my kids and recumbent wife. I cleaned the kitchen, got the kids to sleep, and carried my wife – stoned on

Benadryl – to bed.

I put on a black turtleneck, a stocking cap, and tucked my pant legs into some socks. And then, at midnight, I went to the front door, armed to the hilt.

Slowly, I stepped out and pulled the front door closed behind me. Quiet as an assassin, I waited for my eyes to adjust to the heart of darkness.

Above me, they slept. Or watched Letterman. Whatever wasps do late at night.

I lifted the spray can. Drawing a long, steadying breath, I closed one eye, took aim and squeezed.

Insecticide hissed like a missile. Direct hit!

Instantly, they emerged to dive-bomb me. I sprayed for as long as I could, then whirled and grabbed the door knob.

Uh-oh.

Locked myself out.

Sprinting like Carl Lewis, I made for the street, stopping only at the mailboxes at the end of the block. I stood stock still, heart pounding like the drums in "George of the Jungle's" theme song, and braced for the onslaught.

Nothing. They had lost my trail.

I waited awhile, then cautiously made my way to the side gate, through the back yard and in the back door. Safe inside, I fell into a fitful sleep.

Morning dawned quietly. I peeped out the window by the front door. Nothing was moving. I opened the door a crack. Still nothing moving. I pushed my head out and looked up at the nest. No signs of life.

Did I feel good? Did my face flush and my fist clench with the machismo of a conquering warrior?

No – a wave of guilt washed over me. Geez, what have I done? Slaughtered them as they slept! I'm no better than Custer.

I ambled forlornly out to fetch the Sunday paper.

Bam! He got me on the toe. One brave little straggler, a refugee lurking in the grass.

I limped back inside, got the Benadryl and propped my throbbing purple plum of a toe up on the sofa.

"Honey!" I called. "What's for breakfast?"

Going to the Well for Perspective

Sometimes you watch the great dramas of our times unfold as they have in Florida for the past week, and you're riveted to your chair by the weight of it all.

But then other times, the real world comes calling and makes it all seem painfully irrelevant. There's nothing like a truly crappy day to put national politics in perspective.

Take Tuesday. Please.

Take my wife while you're at it. She's on the phone. It's early on a busy day. I'm editing and she's at home in the mountains outside Placerville, preparing for an important meeting, dripping wet and sudsy with shampoo.

"There's no water," she says.

My stomach lining begins doing origami.

That's the way it is with wells. When you live in the country, there's something essentially gratifying about drawing water from your own well. But there's also something essentially mortifying about turning the spigot when nothing comes out. You can't pick up the phone and call some civil servant, other than your spouse.

"OK," I say. "Stay calm. Go out to the pump house."

She curses into the cordless as she walks with sudsy hair in chilly air 100 yards to the well pump. She opens the door and stares inside at a metropolis of yellow-jacket nests and black widow webs.

"OK, there's a little box with a lever doodad sticking out," I explain, using technical terms. "The lever doodad needs to be flipped from 9 o'clock to 11 o'clock."

"What? 9 o'clock? What are you talking about?"

After a tense repartee, she is able to restart the well pump. She walks back, turns on the faucet and – voila!

I feel gratified and oh so manly. For about an hour. Then my phone rings again. "There's no water," she says.

There is nothing else to do but head home. And mind you, there are only two things I hate more than crawling around with yellow jackets and black widows, and those are working with electricity and plumbing. And mind you again, my well is a hieroglyphic tangle of pumps, diaphragms and gauges powered by no less than 220 volts.

Grimacing, I climb in. Four confusing hours and $30 later, as darkness falls in the woods, I put the finishing touches on my installation of a new pressure regulator and gauge. I turn the faucet. Voila!

Manly gratification washes over me in almost erotic waves. I have fixed my well. I have conquered my fears. I have provided water from my land to my family.

Two hours later, a daughter steps out of the shower.

"There's no water," she says.

Limp with defeat, I trudge into the cold night, climb into the infested pump house and restart the well. I come back and turn the faucet. But this time, no voila.

I call the well-pump guy – a wonderful, patient businessman named Rob who dispenses free advice at night.

"It sounds like your well is going dry," he says.

"What?" I gasp. "How can that be? It's been raining. How can it be dry?"

"I don't know, but a lot of wells have been drying up this year."

We discuss solutions. I'll need to either drill deeper for about $5,000 and uncertain prospects, or put in a holding tank for about $2,500 that can store any water which happens to pass by.

Stunned, I waddle forlornly through the house, only dimly aware of where I am going, until the shock of cold water on my bare feet slaps me into consciousness.

The washing machine has overflowed. It has malfunctioned and refuses to stop filling with water for the spin cycle. I start bailing out water and pouring it down the drain, pierced by the irony that what little water my well is able to produce must now be flushed.

That's enough for one day. Whimpering, I go to bed.

At about 3 a.m. I dream that my finger is throbbing with pain. I awake to discover that my arm is wedged between the bed and the wall and that, indeed, my finger is throbbing with pain. Something – a spider, I guess – has bitten my goddamned finger!

I lay there with my finger throbbing, pierced by the irony that I escaped being bitten by a spider in the pump house only to be bitten as I slept in my bed.

Dawn comes and I am awakened by my daughter.

"There's no water," she says. My slippers crunch across frozen ground as I restart the well and head back inside, where I soon discover that a toilet valve is now malfunctioning, refusing to shut off and sucking up what little water my well is able to produce. It is logical to extrapolate that my septic tank will soon fill up and purge its contents, filling every room in the house.

Which, right about now, would be just fine with me.

And so at moments such as these, with your well dry and your washer broken and your toilet broken and your finger too swollen to pick your nose and your septic tank about to back up and fill your house with excrement – at times like these, national politics seem not to matter.

And therein lies the rub. Because as sure as that septic tank stinks, the second I turn my back, the Rube Goldberg law of governmental chain reaction will kick in and somebody's going to get elected and appoint somebody else who will appoint somebody else who's going to send a memo which begets 3,237 other memos which trigger new regulations which will be interpreted by some local bureaucrat to mean that I need a permit to fix my well.

You can't lose sight of the big picture.

First of All, Avoid Embarrassment

Life is full of defining moments. A few of the unforgettable ones shape us, it is said, changing the way we think and live. They crystallize in our memories: the sound of a grandparent's soothing voice, your first kiss, what you were doing on the morning of Sept. 11.

But I say, if you really want to know which moments shape us, forget the unforgettable ones.

The defining moments that really shape us are the ones that do not linger. We get rid of them as quickly as possible. We hope they won't define us, but they do.

They are our moments of profound embarrassment.

Something protective pushes them into the back of our psyches. They are too painful to recollect. But they shape us more than the moments we remember.

You see, Grasshopper, life is a constant adjustment to avoid embarrassment.

At about the same time Neil Armstrong was walking on the moon, I was walking with the beautiful Gail Seidman across a supermarket parking lot. I was proudly showing her the project I had made in wood shop. She was smiling – promisingly, I might add. At that instant, my brother pulled up in his car and asked if I wanted a ride home. I ran toward his car. But I tripped over a concrete parking lot divider and splayed out, landing on my face. My brother screeched away laughing, and Gail Seidman decided I was not qualified to be her boyfriend.

In that instant, the blueprint for all my relationships with women was set. Essentially it has been one long effort to avoid embarrassment. Skip ahead to a time shortly after the fall of Saigon. At that point in my career, I often took my lunch in a small cafe across the street from my newspaper office. I'd sit, eat and read there so often it became like a second home to me. Until one crowded day in the cafe, while deeply immersed in a tuna sandwich and a John Nichols novel, I absentmindedly farted.

Ultimately I had to leave that town.

Which brought me to the forest home where I live, and the events of last weekend.

Aside from having farted out loud in a restaurant, I live in the mountains because once upon a time I was part of a movement – the 1970s movement away from the smoggy, stinky cities and out to the countryside.

Over the last decade, the movement has been back to the cities. And I know why: wells and septic tanks.

When you live in the country, instead of simply turning a knob and receiving all the water you could possibly want from some municipal service, you must be responsible for pumping your own water up through the earth's crust.

On the converse side of the equation, rather than simply flushing a toilet and watching the ultimate fruits of your labor careen down into a government-operated sewage line (unless you live in Folsom, in which case it ends up in a public park), when you live in the country you must dedicate a good deal of your affluence to seeing that your effluence goes underground into a tank of your own keeping, and from there leaches peacefully and without incident or publicity into the surrounding woodlands.

It's a very good feeling, usually, pumping your own water up from the earth and then, conversely, you know … It's a feeling that grounds you, that lets you know what kind of stuff you're made of, who your grandparents were, and why you shop at REI.

Anyway, it's a very good feeling until things go wrong. And then, at any given moment on any given day, you run the risk of experiencing one of life's truly defining moments – the embarrassing ones.

Last year, on a day that shall live in infamy, my well started going dry. I managed to nurse it along until now, when I could afford to have a gigantic (and incurably ugly) water tank installed next to my well, where I can store whatever water my well happens to capture.

A week ago, shortly before the crew was coming to install my tank, I decided that I should do the crew a favor and tear down the old pump house. It was practically falling down anyway.

And so, at approximately the time anthrax was being distributed free of charge through the U.S. mail, my wife and I began to tear down the shed.

Building things can be satisfying, but for instant gratification nothing beats demolition work.

We quickly pried off the rotting old doors, yanked out nails, and pried off the the decayed plywood siding. I disassembled some of the 220-volt electrical connections. Then we cut through a couple of support braces. We worked carefully so as not to bump into the narrow, 4-foot-tall tank that pressurizes the water in our system.

"Careful now," I said. "We don't want to knock over this pressure tank." "OK," she said. "Let's be careful."

In less than an hour, just a skeleton of the pump house remained. "Gee, you know, we could just push this thing over now," I said.

And so we pushed. And, of course, we knocked over the pressure tank. And about four pipes broke. And a geyser of water shot up into the air. And my wife started laughing. And I had to walk over to my neighbor's house, dripping wet, to ask for help figuring out how to put my well back together again.

And he gave me the same look he gave me the last time I couldn't figure out how to put my well back together.

And it's clear, one of us is going to have to move.

Management Tips from Merry Old Oz

It was when the stage caught on fire that I realized not everything is merry in the Land of Oz.

Back in July, both of my kids got into a community theater production of "The Wizard of Oz." The show finally ended last week. For reasons I can no longer comprehend, last summer I agreed to be the stage manager.

Now, after 26 performances and countless rehearsals … After overseeing a cast of 56 people – 48 of them under the age of 20 – plus a dog … After managing a show with nearly 200 set changes or prop movements …

Now, after all that, the only words of wisdom I can offer are "I'd turn back if I were you."

I had no idea what I was getting into. As soon as I began attending rehearsals in October, a month before opening night, it became clear I was in over my head.

The sets were huge, clunky wooden contraptions. We would have only seconds to get them on and off the stage between scenes, using two big turntables. Backstage, there was barely enough space for all the stuff. Every move had to be choreographed precisely, or else we were going to squish some Munchkins.

It was dark and disorienting backstage. I didn't know what went where or when. We weren't in Kansas anymore.

It took me weeks to analyze and assign all the split-second movements. Late at night, after rehearsals, I would sit at a computer and try to decipher my notes. A new set of cheat sheets would be produced, only to realize the next night that I was still wrong in a half-dozen spots.

The idea that I'd get to spend more time with my kids quickly evaporated. I rushed past them occasionally in the darkness. "Hi, Dad," they would whisper, dopplering away from me before I could ask if their homework was done.

Other little kids would tug on my sleeve. "The director says to ask if you need help," they'd say. "Yeah," I'd reply. "Run to the store and get me some Rolaids."

It was not until opening night that we actually pulled it off – and even then, a couple of painted backdrops got mixed up, making it look as if Uncle Henry's farm had been subdivided by real estate developers.

But after a few shows, it was going smoothly. The stage and lighting crews were casually exchanging dirty jokes on our headsets. As they say in theater, we had us a show.

Then came our first Sunday matinee. I nonchalantly set up one of the show's two explosive charges, used when the Wicked Witch throws flame balls at the Scarecrow. Perhaps, in retrospect, I used too much flash powder.

Suddenly, an urgent voice from the light booth came over my headset. "We have a fire on the set! This is not a drill! The stage is on fire!"

I squinted at the fuzzy black-and-white TV monitor backstage. Sure enough, there was a 2-foot ball of flame leaping from a piece of silk. Lion was trying to put it out with his paws, and Dorothy was swinging her basket at it.

We got the fire out. Nobody broke character. The show barely missed a beat. My heart, however, was missing more beats that the Tin Man's.

A few days later came the First Dog Episode. "Toto's slipped his leash!" came the voice on my headset. "He's wandering loose on the stage! He's headed stage right!"

I flopped on my belly and waited in the wings for the dog to come around the corner. Imagine his surprise when my hand reached out of the darkness and yanked him off the stage.

Then came the Second Dog Episode. The show was about to start. Uncle Henry and Aunt Em were onstage, counting chickens. Dorothy was supposed to rush up the center aisle with Toto in her arms, but she was nowhere to be seen. Aunt Em and Henry were up to 55 chickens. No Dorothy.

"Toto's slipped his leash!" came the voice in my headset. "He's loose in the audience!"

The next minutes churned slowly in the dark theater. First you'd hear the dog yelp, and then you'd hear humans yelp as lunging stage hands grabbed audience members by their ankles. Up on stage, Em and Henry were up to 76 chickens by the time we recaptured Toto.

Then came the Great Peanut Butter Episode. By the 15th show, Toto had started to really ham it up, trying to bite the Lion and yapping at everything that moved.

To quiet him down, I started slathering peanut butter in strategic spots. He'd get it in his mouth and couldn't bark. If I timed it right, he'd shut up during the quiet parts, and he'd resume barking during the action scenes.

It worked like a charm for four shows in a row. But midway through a Sunday matinee, Toto suddenly slumped to the floor with a pained expression on his face. He wouldn't budge. Scarecrow had to carry him around for the rest of the show.

We took Toto to the vet the next day. The dog was profoundly constipated. I had shut him up at both ends.

Then came the Munchkin Poisoning Episode, which I probably shouldn't go into for reasons of civil liability. Suffice it to say that when you are blowing fire extinguishers up the skirts of wicked witches for special effect, it is important to know that some fire extinguishers use harmless CO_2, and others use noxious chemicals that can require entire theaters to be evacuated.

It is over now. I can look back and sift through my experience as a stage manager. And I can tell you this:

It ain't gonna happen again.

The World's Safe-Sexiest Automobile

In the past I have said and written many disparaging things about the 1985 Ford Escort Model L automobile. In particular, I have said nasty things about my 1985 Ford Escort Model L automobile, which, as they say in the Bible, sucketh mightily.

In the parking lot just now, however, I had a revelation. Verily, it causeth me to reconsider all those nasty things I've said. Maybe I've been too harsh.

It occurs to me that the Escort is an asset in this crime-ridden age. Not because it is a good car, but precisely because it is a terrible car.

Nobody wants to steal a 1985 Ford Escort Model L.

Nobody.

The Ford Escort, therefore, is clearly one of the safest cars on the road.

There were 20-some-odd thousand carjackings in this great nation last year. I know, because I watched a TV news magazine. It's an urban fad. But I'll reckon none of those carjackings involved a 1985 Ford Escort Model L.

I am safe, therefore, at any intersection in the worst, most run-down, trickled-down neighborhoods of America. I can sit there at any stop light with the Escort trying its best to idle, and I can feel secure.

Nobody is going to walk up to my car, shove stubby fingers into my face (thieves always have stubby fingers; it's a sign of their caste) and say, "Your Escort or your life!"

The 1985 Escort Model L is not worth the trouble.

Will the Escort be stolen by burglars? Oh, come on. Conduct an experiment. Imagine you're a thief like your ancestors, you have stubby fingers that cannot play the piano, write poetry or count money with any degree of dexterity. Walk into a parking lot and look around. What are you going to steal?

Not an Escort.

You'll see plenty of cars you can't steal, because their owners have put those Club anti-theft devices on the steering wheels: Saabs, BMWs, Lexuses, even my fellow journalist's 1960 Impala, for cryin' out loud. They've all got The Club.

As an Escort owner, I am not required to buy The Club because the stubby-fingered thieves are going to steal something else – that Toyota 4Runner, maybe, or the Isuzu Trooper with the environmentalist bumper sticker. The Ford Ranger for sure.

Unless I am so stupid as to leave a leather jacket or some other valuable item on the front seat, I can slide through life without being the victim of auto-related violent crime.

Which is not to say I won't be the victim of some sort of larceny, such as the kind performed by transmission shops.

But unless I physically attack the owner of the transmission shop, get arrested and then raped in jail, the Escort prevents me from being victimized by violent crime.

The Escort, therefore, is one of the safest cars on the road.

Insurance companies should pay me for driving an Escort, the way I pay mechanics for the privilege of keeping the sucker on the road. (The Escort is into me for $2,750 so far this year, and counting.)

Don't let anybody tell you that the 1985 Ford Escort Model L automobile is a mere Pinto in disguise. It's much more than that.

The Escort, which somebody told me is the best-selling car in the whole world, also can attract women.

That's right.

The Escort is a sex symbol.

This latest revelation came to me – surged over me, really, the way an epiphany surges over a monk – while I was watching a TV commercial for Hyundai.

The commercial shows several male models pulling up to the curb in expensive and sporty cars – BMWs, Saabs, Corvettes. On the sidewalk, female models mock them, figuring the expensive and sporty cars are a sure sign of male arrogance and/or compensation for anatomical "shortcomings."

Then a fellow drives up in his dull little Hyundai and the women know, instinctively, that here's a man who really knows how to perform sex.

Well, if a Hyundai has become some sort of sexual status symbol, then a 1985 Ford Escort Model L amounts to an out-and-out aphrodisiac.

It's amazing that I haven't been mobbed at the curb outside the Rubicon Brewery by hungry women looking for a down-to-earth guy who's so self-confident he drives a 1985 Ford Escort Model L.

In fact, the more I think about it, the more nervous all this makes me.

Clearly, it's only a matter of time before I am mobbed at every curb by women – burning, yearning women who take karate classes and carry Mace – merely because I drive a 1985 Ford Escort Model L

Hmmmmm.

Guess the Escort isn't so safe after all.

Costa Rican Pizza

Tales From the Heart

Post-Vacation Claustrophobic Blues

It was while fiddling with my key chain on Monday morning that the post-vacation claustrophobic blues hit.

I woke up bright and early and forgot for a moment that I was no longer in the Hawaiian Islands. Four weeks of vacation – my longest stretch of time off since 1975 – had surged over me like a warm ocean. Now it was time to go to work, and I needed to sort out my keys.

Three keys had been taken with me to Hawaii, three had been left with my housesitter, and about five stayed home in a drawer. They needed to be reunited on a single key chain, but it was dumbfounding. I stared at them. What are all these things for? There's one for my car, three for the office building, one for the file cabinet, my house, my garage, my gates. But what's this one for? And this one?

And why does my life involve so many locks?

As I stare, jangling the keys, a cloud passes over and just for a moment the sound becomes the jangling anchor chain of a sailboat …

Her name is Pauroa, a Tahitian word that means having one's life in order. She's a 45-foot trimaran moored just inside a reef on the sweet east end of Molokai. The water there glistens and winks, the color of Elizabeth Taylor's eyes.

We stayed a week in a guest cottage on the property of Pauroa's owners. It was a paradise of morning glories and papaya trees and vines that flower at night. My daughters spent the time gathering seashells. My wife and I spent the week gazing longingly at Pauroa.

Pauroa is fast – she once sailed from Tahiti to Molokai in 11 days. Her three hulls are spacious – large enough for a family of four to live on. And she's for sale – just $20,000. That's a steal.

Should we? We agonize over this opportunity. We could sell the house, buy the boat and have enough to live on for a year or two. Would we?

The memory gets away. I sort my keys and head out the door. The day is cold and stormy. A cherry tree fights to bloom. Yesterday, it was 80 degrees and papaya juice was dripping from my chin. Another reverie sweeps me away, and just for a moment the cherry tree becomes a coconut palm swaying on the South Kona coast. ...

We met a family that bought an acre of beach on the Big Island, cleared it with machetes, put in solar electricity and were building a cluster of homes straight out of Robinson Crusoe. Thatched roofs by weavers from Tonga. Bamboo rafters, open to the ocean in front, gardens in back.

The couple building it are travel photographers, They have a 5-year-old daughter who every afternoon swims with dolphins about 100 yards offshore.

They ask us if we'd like to build a thatched-roof house on the property and live there as caretakers. I could write books. My daughters could swim with dolphins. The only catch is, we have to have an answer by next week.

Could we? Ideas march up boldly, then sneak away. ...

The next thing I know, I'm driving into downtown Sacramento, wearing a necktie and black leather shoes that belong on a mortician. Somebody in a Mercedes tries to run me off N Street, and another scene overtakes me. ...

We're on the little road that leads to an acre of land my wife owns on the calm southwestern flank of Mauna Loa. The land is overgrown, but I see its possibilities. I'd clear a driveway right through here. Toward the front of the property I'd build a small guest house. We'd live in it while I built the big house, back there, with an ocean view.

The man across the road is 69 years old. For 14 years, he and his wife have lived in a rustic cabin while they built, entirely by hand, a lava-rock house on top of the hill. It's 3,000 square feet, his masterpiece, his obsession. The gardens are hers, a paradise of orchids and plumeria.

They hope to live in the house before they die. The volcano doesn't worry them. After all, lava hasn't flowed through this neighborhood since 1950.

We could take the caretaking job up the coast and I could build on weekends. My wife could work nights. We could live beneath the volcano, too. ...

Suddenly I'm at my desk looking at a stack of mail.

Why do we do this to ourselves? Why do we go traveling and

tempt ourselves with the fruit of the world?

It's a reward system. We see life offers more than work, and it makes the work easier. We know the Pauroa is there by the reef; maybe someday we can afford it. If we blow out, the caretaker's job waits like an escape hatch. Someday we can retire to our acre beneath the volcano. The risk in this reward system, however, is insanity's second cousin, the post-vacation claustrophobic blues.

Post-vacation claustrophobic blues can be managed, however. The key, of course, is to measure it accurately. There are two formulas for calculation.

The first formula measures the depth of the blues. Multiply the number of days of your vacation by pi. A five-day vacation is calculated thus: 5 X 3.14159 = 15.7. That's roughly the turquoise hue of a Caribbean lagoon. My 27-day vacation left me with a depth factor of 84.82, which is the color of the ocean off Newfoundland in November.

Should long vacations therefore be avoided? No no no. Our second measurement – the duration of post-vacation claustrophobic blues – has an inverse and overriding effect. The longer your vacation, the shorter your blues.

To calculate the duration of your PVCB, subtract your depth factor from the number of days in the year, then multiply that number by 365, and then multiply that number by pi. This gives you the number of minutes you'll have PVCB. (There are 1,440 minutes in a day.)

The duration of post-vacation claustrophobic blues after a five-day trip is 278 days. The duration of blues after a 27-day trip is a mere 223 days.

This may seem a small and dismaying disparity. But note that there are a total of 260 working days in a year. (most of us aren't affected by PVCB on weekends, unless we get sucked into the office.) So if we're only taking weeklong vacations, we're actually accruing 18 days of blues a year. If we take monthlong vacations, we'll be working 37 highly productive days a year without the blues.

It's difficult for your boss to argue with science. This formula will make it a lot easier to make a case for the monthlong vacation you want to take instead of the weeklong vacation your boss wants you to take.

Hey, we're here to help.

Bite by Bite, a Dad's Power Melts

I am sitting on the sofa, wondering when it was exactly that I lost all credibility with my kids.

My younger daughter is standing on her head in the hallway. She thinks it will make her taller.

If I tell her she's probably wasting her time and ought to be doing her algebra, she won't believe me.

My older daughter is mentally reliving her latest hair-raising episode behind the wheel of my car. She's been learning to drive. It doesn't matter to her if I urge her to slow down, to not be in such a hurry, and that she ought to be thinking about what's around the next bend. After all, I don't know what I'm talking about.

In the last six months, this sense that Dad is full of it – a know-it-all who doesn't know anything at all – has permeated the household. They even have a saying for it. It goes like this:

"Lauren, standing on your head won't make you taller."

"That's Costa Rican pizza, Dad."

"Rachel, slow down for this blind curve. There's a highly explosive propane truck ahead."

"That's Costa Rican pizza, Dad."

And that's when it comes back to haunt to me – the exact moment when I lost all credibility with my kids. I drift back to last July ...

... We have been in Costa Rica only a few days when we walk into a small roadside cafe in the town of Quepos. Rachel is a bit homesick, so her eyes light up when she sees pizza on the menu.

"What do you think Costa Rican pizza is like, Dad?"

"Well, I don't know." I clear my throat and furrow my brow. "This is an entirely different culture. You can get a lot of variation from one country to another in the definition of 'pizza.' It might be that the restaurant is trying to curry favor with Americans by putting it on the menu, but you might find it's not much more than –"

"Dad, do you think I ought to order the pizza?"

"Sure, go ahead. Just be forewarned that it might not meet your expectations of what a pizza is or ought to be."

So the rest of us order typical Costa Rican food – fish, rice and beans – and Rachel orders the pizza.

Pretty soon, the waiter comes to the table and puts a plate in front of her. On the plate is a round, pan-fried loaf of what looks very much like pita bread, and a small bowl of a cream that looks very much like pesto.

She looks at it. She looks at me. I smile knowingly.

"Costa Rican pizza," I pronounce.

She picks up a wedge of the bread, eyes it warily, dips it in the sauce and takes a bite. "Hey, it's pretty good."

The rest of us ask for a bite. We all agree. This Costa Rican pizza is weird, but it's good. We reach across the table to grab for more.

"No, hey, stay away," she says, swatting our hands. "This is my lunch. Wait for your own food."

While we wait, she scarfs down the Costa Rican pizza. We're all starving, drooling for something to eat, admiring her quickly disappearing food from across the table.

"You were right, Dad," she says, polishing off the last piece, pushing away from the table, full to the brim. "They sure do make pizza different down here. It's good, though."

I smile the Father Knows Best smile. The one I have been getting away with for exactly 14 years, four months and 22 days.

Now the waiter reappears.

He plops down plates of fish, rice and beans for the rest of us. And then, with a flourish, he places before Rachel a steaming, classic pepperoni pizza.

There is a prolonged moment of silence.

We all stare at the pizza. Their eyes all turn to me. They turn back to the pizza. I can only blink.

"Costa Rican pizza, huh, Dad?"

And that was that.

For the next three weeks, as we explored jungles and oceans, the phrase "Costa Rican pizza" tormented me.

We rode horses and I was forbidden from offering advice on how to mount, turn or canter.

"That's Costa Rican pizza, Dad."

We watched volcanoes and I was prohibited from explaining the nuances of magma or tectonic plates.

"That's Costa Rican pizza, Dad."

When we went into the surf near a river mouth, my warnings that crocodiles sometimes appear amid the waves in this part of the world went unheeded.

"That's Costa Rican pizza, Dad."

Always with a roll of the eyes. Always with a tone of mocking dismissal. Always with a thinly cloaked disdain for this doddering, pontificating old sperm-donor of a dad.

We returned home, and my hopes that they would surrender the phrase at the Customs desk were dashed. Again and again, it keeps creeping up. A euphemism for blowhardiness – a painful reminder that once, in a small Central American town, I mistook an appetizer of pita bread and pesto sauce for an Italian baked dish consisting of a shallow pie crust covered usually with a spiced mixture of tomatoes, cheese and other toppings.

I had been wrong. But worse, I had been wrong with an air of absolute certainty that I was right.

Try teaching a teenager to drive – let alone telling one to stop standing on her head and do her algebra – when they think you're full of Costa Rican pizza.

A Meeting at Kings County Airport, 1961

I met Santa Claus when I was 7 years old. He has stayed with me ever since.

If you scoff, it's only because part of your brain has hardened up.

It was 1961. The Kings County Airport wasn't much of a facility, just a little general aviation airport out in the boonies near Hanford. You wouldn't expect to meet Santa there.

My old man had a pilot's license and had rented a small plane. Ostensibly we were on a business trip. He worked as an engineer for an aerospace company in Southern California and had clients to see up north. But the real reason for the trip was to get the family up to see Grandma and Grandpa in Stockton for Christmas.

It was the start of Christmas break, just a few days before the holiday, and we were flying at night.

Try to imagine the magic that goes through a 7-year-old child's head as he gazes out the window of a small plane that's motoring northward just a few nights before Christmas. Try to picture what he's looking for among the stars.

At 7, I reckon I was tottering on that cusp of faith that beckons a child at about that age. Intellectually, I knew by then that Santa was a mythological character. We find out from school friends and through osmosis far too soon.

But you don't quite believe what you're hearing. Certainly, you don't want to believe it. You want to know that magic exists in this world. And intuitively, you know Santa embodies that magic. But all around you are nonbelievers, pushing you toward the cusp of faith.

In fact, looking back to even earlier days, I recall that my father always told me Santa was a myth, even when I was tiny. He told his kids it had crushed him when he was a child to find out there was no Santa, so he didn't want us to be crushed that way.

Luckily, I never believed Dad. I figured it was just him being moody around the holidays. I felt sorry for him because he didn't know there was a Santa Claus. Part of his brain had hardened.

And so it came to pass that I was peering through the windows of a Cessna airplane on a clear December night, looking hard among the stars, hoping to catch a glimpse of the sleigh being taken out for a shakedown flight.

We were hungry so we stopped at the Kings County Airport and went into the small cafe there. We weren't the only people in the cafe. It was fairly busy.

I remember a white-haired old man eating alone at the counter. He wore a gray flannel suit, was slight of build and had glasses. Nothing was special about him. But at one point, between arguments at the dinner table with my older brother and sister, my eyes met those of the old man's. And it made him smile.

I can still remember that I had shrimp. I always had shrimp. "Shrimp for a shrimp," my big brother would jeer as he slavered through a burger.

Big brothers can be merciless. Who knows what mine would have done if he had guessed I'd been looking for Santa that night. He probably would have noogied my scalp until his knuckles bled.

We finished eating and were waiting for the check when all of a sudden there was a tap on my shoulder.

I turned and looked up. It was the old man. His white hair framed a kind face.

"Excuse me, young man," he said, extending his hand, "but I just wanted to shake your hand."

I was startled, but his smile and the twinkle in his eye put me at ease. The whole table went silent and I could feel the eyes of my family bulging in my direction.

"Sure," I said, and held out my hand.

He put something there as we shook.

"A dollar!" I exclaimed, opening my palm.

"Five dollars!" I shouted again as I uncrumpled the bill. Remember this was 1961, and $5 could set up a 7-year-old kid financially for months.

"Thanks, mister!" I said, looking up and expecting him to still be standing there.

But he was already walking out the door, heading into the cold December night with a spring in his step.

"Mom, he gave me five dollars! Should I go after him and thank him?"

"No, honey, it's all right," she said, her hand on my shoulder.

She was following him out the door with her eyes, not suspiciously, but with an air of gentle sympathy.

Being a parent now, I know what she was thinking. Surely, this man must have lost a son – someone who looked a lot like her own son. The holidays were bearing down on him. He was aching in loneliness. And somehow, giving to a child for the simple and pure joy of giving was a way to rekindle his own spirit.

That was a reasonable conclusion. And intellectually, right then and there, I reached the same conclusion myself. He had lost a child. He wanted to remember what joy looked like.

But our minds, thank God, are more than mere intellectual contraptions.

Somewhere in there between the thalamus, the cerebellum and the medulla oblongata, there is a sacred place between the mind and the soul and the heart. It is the place where wisdom and intuition reside. When we take care not to let it harden over, it gives us the capacity to embrace magic, myth and faith, and to make them a part of our reality.

And I knew in that place, between the mind and the soul and the heart, that I had just shaken hands with Santa Claus.

And I know it still.

Aging Gracefully Requires Adventure

A couple of weeks ago, I unabashedly asked you, gentle reader, to send me cards and presents in order to stop me from whining about my 40th birthday.

I got two cards.

Now, that's not exactly an outpouring of support. And after all I've done for you! I would be plenty upset about this – and I would find some way to get even – except that my wife got all of you off the hook.

You all owe her a debt of gratitude, if not cards and presents.

So here's the way it went down. She took me out to dinner on Friday night, five days before my birthday and gave me a plane ticket to Mexico. A complete out-of-the blue surprise.

"You're leaving tomorrow," she said, "and you'd better have a good time and stop whining."

I figured that was the least I could do.

My sister-in-law was at the same dinner. She gave my brother a plane ticket to Mexico, too, since both of us celebrate our birthday on the same day. (Not twins, just three years apart. I also have sisters who are precisely three years apart, to the day. I figure dad came into heat at regular intervals.)

So the next day — taking advantage of an act of generosity that can only be appreciated if you know how long it has been since I had the dough to take my wife on a decent vacation — my brother and I flew to Cabo San Lucas to grow old in exile.

Allow me to recommend the following formula for turning 40 without giving a damn about it:

Start by drinking lots of margaritas the moment you arrive at a hotel bar in Mexico until you make friends with every gringo there. Then make plans with them to do every goofy thing imaginable.

For example, make arrangements to rent dirt bikes the next morning. Then go out drinking that night and repeatedly lift your glasses to say (in a gruff, Treasure of the Sierra Madre accent) "Tonight we drink, for tomorrow we ride!"

Hauling butt across Baja sand dunes on a non-Sierra Club-approved dirt bike is not only a great cure for a hangover, it also is the easiest and quickest way to feel 11 years old again.

And feeling 11 years old again is a fine way to forget that you are soon to turn 40.

After your ride, drink more margaritas until you fall face-down on the beach. Wake up in mid-afternoon and drag yourself to a hot tub that faces the setting sun.

After dark, round up your new gringo friends and go out for another night of drinking. Find a place where people dance on table tops, and where men who are dressed to look like banditos grab you by the scalp, jerk your head back, pour tequila shooters down your throat and then shake your head violently for a 60-cent service charge.

If you have not yet stopped whining about your birthday, then on your second day, eat breakfast while watching an eclipse of the sun over the veranda. Then go buy something in the marketplace for your spouse. Haggle vigorously with the vendors, as if saving 20 cents were going to make a difference. Then pay five times true value for the ugliest pair of parrot-shaped earrings ever made.

After your shopping expedition, go snorkeling until you are content enough to spend the afternoon in siesta. Wake up when it is time to go drinking again.

This time, find a bar where you can be hung upside down by your ankles so that banditos can pour more tequila down your throat.

Once this hanging upside down has happened to you, you won't mind it so much when a one-eyed psychopathic local challenges you to a knife fight in the street. "Tonight you die!" he screams in your face. "Oh yeah?" you scream back, before somebody drags you both away.

After behaving this way until 3 in the morning, wake up at 5 and go climb aboard a fishing boat. Without breakfast, without coffee, popping Dramamine like they were Pez, go fishing for the giant striped marlin.

An hour out on the Sea of Cortez, your crew sets up the lures and you begin to troll for the giant trophy fish that is the symbol of all that is good and right and true in every Hemingway bad-writing contest.

When you have been sitting for an hour in one of the swivel chairs used to catch fish, and just as the trolling begins, you must excuse yourself to go use the head.

A gringo vacation buddy named Marty from Portland will sit in your chair and immediately fall asleep. Fifteen minutes later, the giant marlin will hit, suddenly and ferociously, true and good like the bull at Pamplona.

The fishing guides will hook it, and they will shake Marty awake and put a fishing pole in his hands with a 125-pound marlin on the end of the line. He will spend the next hour and 15 minutes having the adventure of his life, catching the fish that would have been yours if you hadn't gone to use the john.

Spend the rest of the day not catching any marlin, but laughing about everything until your stomach hurts.

Fail to remember that this morning is, in fact, your 40th birthday …

These are the things you must do in order to age gracefully.

But in order to have these things happen to you – and here's the tough part – you must be married to someone as good and right and true as my wife.

Fat chance.

Of Mothers and Others
in the Loom

I think sometimes that we humans, down there in the DNA, carry bits and scraps of the accumulated experiences of our ancestors.

Genetic memories float beneath the surface of our conscious minds, bobbing up in certain currents, affecting what we do and think and feel.

The part of me that loves the sea is a remnant, maybe, from my seafaring ancestors of Cornwall.

I am innately swept away by the sound of an Irish fiddle, owing perhaps to some ancient Celt in the woodshed.

Running on a treadmill at the health club, sometimes I close my eyes and the rhythmic stamp of my feet suggests moccasins on the forest floor.

I wonder about them, those forgotten ancestors. I wish they weren't forgotten. I wish I knew their stories, these people who affect my preferences, my behavior, the reactions I have to different situations.

Oh, I know a few particulars – names, dates, places. My wife can trace her Swedish side back to the year 1684, but again, it's mostly names, dates, places.

It is a distinctly modern sorrow that so few of us know their stories – the way they toiled, the risks they took, their dreams and desires. That is, except for what is remembered down in the DNA.

The longer ago it was, the thinner the thread.

If threads of DNA connect us to our forebears, then the opposite must be true of those to whom we are closest.

And closest of all are the ties between a mother and her children. These aren't thread; they're something like steel cables, I think.

I don't know how much of a mother's bond to her children has to do with genetics, and how much comes from the tremendous responsibility a parent accepts. Certainly adoptive parents love their children no less than biological ones, and in some cases far more. But still, I am drawn back to the notion that there is something we don't fully understand about our genetic ties.

I drove to work this morning thinking about mothers: my mom, my wife, my sisters. And I wondered about the kinds of mothers that my daughters could someday grow up to be.

A happy memory came drifting by:

I was a 10-year-old kid, already an avid little surfer. (Egads! He's telling surf stories again.) For me and all of my friends, my mom was the driver of the surf wagon. Nearly every weekend for the following three or four years, she would drive us up and down the coastline, looking for waves and surf spots.

She was such a good sport. Sometimes we would insist on surfing at places like Cotton's Point or Black's, where you had to hike more than a mile, up and down cliffs, to reach the waves. She never hesitated. She hiked beside us, and while we were in the water, she blissfully strolled the beach, watching our every movement.

I knew she loved those days. Later I came to know that those were days of freedom for her – freedom from the humdrum of her second failing marriage.

Recently, my own 10-year-old, Rachel, engaged me in a conversation that taught me another side of what my mom must have felt during those days on the beach – a side that goes much deeper.

"Dad, how old will I be in the '50s?" Rachel asked.

It took a second to sink in: She was asking how old she will be in the year 2050.

"You'll be in your 60s," I said. "And if you had tried, young lady, you could have done the math yourself."

She brushed past my moralizing. "How old will my kid be?"

"In the year 2050? Your kid will probably be in her 30s. Why?"

"How old will my grand kids be?"

"Well, they'll probably be babies."

"Ah nuts," she said. "I always wanted to be a teenager in the '50s."

At first, I giggled.

She had concluded that the next '50s will be just like the last '50s – those historically revised, fun, poodle-skirt 1950s that she's seen in the movies. She's going to be a teenager all too soon, but she's still enough of a child to be able to issue such innocent proclamations.

And then I realized that she had revealed something deeper.

To Rachel, it didn't matter whether it was going to be her, or her child, or her grandchild who got to be a teenager in the '50s. If just one of them got to have the experience, then she would have it.

And here's the thing: I don't think Rachel believes the experience will be vicarious. Rather, she senses it will be virtual – that the psychic connection between a mother and her children transcends time, transcends physical distance, transcends generations.

And I have come to realize that when my mom watched us surf, she wasn't on the beach. She was inside of us. She was flying along those waves with us.

I wonder if mothers feel this more than fathers do. I suppose it depends on the people involved. I do remember cutting the umbilical cord when my second daughter, Lauren, was born, and feeling as if it was the single most intrusive thing I had ever done.

I watch my daughters when they dance ballet and I feel full of pride and wonder.

But when I look over at my wife, I see something beyond pride and wonder in her eyes as she watches them.

I see my wife transported. Her body turns gently into their every pirouette. She flinches at the botched grand jeté, revels in the motion of a well-poised arabesque.

They are her.

Fire in the Forest
Freezes Your Veins

I stood on the ridge and squinted into the night. There, a quarter-mile away – was that the glow of a fire? Yep. There are few glows that are more beautiful and frightening at the same time than the glow of a forest fire at night in the mountains. It's a sight that can make your heart start doing the wa-watusi with your tonsils.

It was last Friday night and the air around my Placerville home was grubby with smoke. The canyons echoed with the sounds of fire trucks far too close.

I hiked back down from the ridge in the dark to my house in Wild Goose Canyon. OK, I said to me, settle down. Process this information. Is your family in danger?

Let's see. The fire is a quarter-mile away. That's bad. But the forest is still pretty green and doesn't burn easily this early in spring. That's good.

The fire has burned about 100 acres and is only 30 percent contained. That's bad. But it has reached a ridgetop, where a fire will often slow itself down. That's good.

There's only one more canyon between the fire and my ridgetop. That's really bad. But the strong winds have died down quite a bit. That's very good.

Now, approaching the cheerful – and suddenly vulnerable – light of our house, I screw on a cheerful face.

"Well?" my wife asks, her lips drawn tight since the smoke first appeared this afternoon, followed by a serenade of helicopters and planes going over the house.

"Oh, you can kind of see the glow," I say. "But I can't really see any flames or anything. It's pretty far out there."

Just to be safe, I add, we ought to take home the two kids who are here to stay the night with ours. What I don't say is how I'm wrestling with whether we should go somewhere else to stay the night ourselves.

"If they tell us to get out, how long do they usually give you?" she asks.

"Half an hour, usually."

"That's not very much time."

"What would we take?" my older daughter asks.

"We'd have to grab what was important, I guess."

"I'm taking my stuffed animals and my turtle," the younger says. "And my piano."

"I'm not too sure about the piano, sweetie."

"The photographs," my wife says. "We would take things that we can't replace with money. The heirlooms. My grandmother's fiddle."

"The hard drive," I say. "It has all our stuff on it."

"A week's worth of clothes," she says.

"The cats," says the oldest. "I'm not leaving the cats."

We fall silent under this grim inventory.

"What about this book you're reading?" She holds up my copy of "Young Men and Fire," which has held me spellbound for a week. It is Norman MacLean's account of 13 smokejumpers who died fighting the Mann Gulch fire in 1949. They parachuted into the mountains of northern Montana to fight what looked like a routine, 100-acre blaze when suddenly there was a "blowup" and the mountain exploded. None but three survived.

"I don't need that book right now," I say. "Besides, I really don't think it's going to come to leaving. It's too green for the fire to keep spreading. And anyway, it's a quarter-mile away."

"A quarter-mile?" she says. "You said it was pretty far out there."

So we decide to pile in the car to take the friends home and see if we can find a vantage point where we can all see the fire. Or maybe we can find a captain to talk to. When you're scared, you want information, and you want to see the thing that scares you.

I never fought forest fires like a lot of my friends did, but I covered a few when I was a young reporter.

The worst one I ever saw was back in 1979. It was called the Chili Bar fire. It consumed thousands of acres and took a week to contain. On the very first night, it began down in the American River canyon, not more than a couple of miles from where I live now. It crowned that night, racing from treetop to treetop, whirling and shaking new fire ahead of itself, creating its own wind.

It raced up to a place called Union Ridge, about a quarter-mile from my mother's house. She got the tap on her door. A sheriff's deputy, saying pack the truck.

But the Chili Bar fire hit the ridge and slowed down. The next morning, the wind changed and blew the fire north to the other side of the river.

I will never forget standing on the deck of my mom's house and staring across the river, watching that fire "blow up" and race up a two-mile mountainside in 15 minutes. When the smoke had cleared an hour later, a lone house on that mountainside was still standing, with a fire truck nearby. I couldn't believe the bravery of that crew or the ferocity of that fire. Few things I have ever seen shook me more deeply.

Now we drive around until we find the makeshift fire headquarters. A captain with the state Department of Forestry puts our minds at ease. It'll be contained by morning, he says, smiling at my girls. It'll be OK.

He takes his hat off, runs an experienced hand through his hair and mumbles a quiet aside.

"Mighty early for this," he says. "We haven't even declared fire season yet. It's going to be a long one."

After 25 Years You Can't Go Home

When we moved last January, my wife and I figured that this new house will someday be the place where our children will return with their own kids. "This is where I grew up," they will say, all misty-eyed. "I used to swing from that tree over there. I used to sit in this corner and read on rainy days."

It's a nice thing to be able to do – to go home again.

I went down to my old stomping grounds on the south Orange County coast recently, where the real estate developers never know when to stop. And I realized that only two things remain unchanged in the 25 years since I moved away. And they are the closest things I have to going home – a seafood joint and a beach.

The south O.C. coast was a wonderland in the '50s and '60s. Empty beaches, air perfumed with ocean and chaparral. Thousands of glimmering days spent exploring the tide pools, surfing the waves, snorkeling the reefs, sailing the winds and warming by the twilight fires.

It was free and clean. You could gather mussels and grunion, boil them in a coffee can and eat 'em right on the beach. There was no polluted runoff from inland places like Irvine and Mission Viejo, because there was no Irvine and Mission Viejo.

Today most of the beaches are regulated and coin-operated, or gated behind mansions, or have sunk beneath the descending masses that I fled in 1974. Boil up a mussel now and they'll either arrest you or hospitalize you.

At Salt Creek, south of Laguna, two little old men lived in a shack on the bluffs. For a buck they let you drive a dirt road down to a pristine beach where seven people were a crowd. You could dive for abalone and surf great waves in water so clear you could see the bottom as you glided.

I can barely look at Salt Creek now. Rooftops stretch as far as the eye can see. Bluffs were bulldozed into the sea to build a Ritz Carlton, forever murking the water. You'd sooner find a unicorn than an abalone.

But a few miles south of Salt Creek is San Onofre. It's on a Marine Corps base, so it has never been developed. It looks today much as it looked back in the 1950s, when it became one of California's classic surf spots, along with Malibu, Windansea and Rincon.

You still take a dirt road down to San-O. They allow only a certain number of vehicles in at a time. That helps keep the crowds down and preserve the feel of the place.

The beach still has palm-thatched shacks put up by the San-O Surf Club before I was born – spots with names like Dawg Patch, Old Man's and The Point. Families still cook in the fire rings. They surf until the sun goes down. They even smile at one another in the water sometimes – just like the old days. It feels like going home.

And then there's the world's best seafood restaurant – The Crab Cooker in Newport Beach.

That's where I go for a home-cooked meal. I always get the same thing – shrimp on a skewer, 22 of 'em, laced with a little bacon and grilled. Served on a paper plate with drawn butter, cheesy potatoes and coleslaw, with a draught Heineken in a plastic cup on the side.

The place hasn't changed for 48 years. It's still in the goofy red building across from Newport Pier. I was 6 when I first went there in 1960 – the year they caught the huge white shark that hangs from the ceiling. The menu is exactly the same, all cooked perfectly, the same way every time – and the prices have no way kept up with inflation.

There isn't any dessert on the menu, and you'd be too full for it anyway.

They don't take reservations. When Nixon was president, hangin' in San Clemente, The Crab Cooker wanted him to stand in line with everyone else. The only way not to stand in line is to go about 3 in the afternoon, like me.

"Eat Lots A Fish." That's the motto. The waitresses still don't mind if you stuff your pockets with breadsticks. The old red tables are still jumbled together with mismatched wooden chairs. A mermaid from some long-sunken prow still reigns on walls cluttered with flotsam and jetsam, from back when Newport was a real fisherman's town.

We had a sailboat – a 32-foot trimaran called the Miraquita that my dad spent five long years building in our back yard. I'll never forget the maiden voyage in 1966 when we launched her from a crane at Long Beach and sailed 20 miles down to her mooring in Newport. We tied her off in the dark and went for a late dinner at The Crab Cooker. That was how every adventure ended.

About 10 years ago, my old man was in the hospital. They had amputated his leg, and they didn't think his ticker was going to hold out. My brother and I arrived to find him conked on morphine. He wouldn't eat anything.

We drove over to The Crab Cooker. Placed an order to-go. Some crab legs and chowder – skip the Heiny.

When we got back to the hospital, we found his old longshoremen buddies gathering, telling stories of the docks. Dad's eyes began to gleam, and he pounded down those crab legs as if they were mother's milk.

He lived another five or six years.

Now that he's gone, the only places to go down there that feel like home are San-O and The Crab Cooker.

"See that seat over there?" I say to my kids. "That's where I sat on the night we sailed the Miraquita home."

Is That the Best
the Moon Can Do?

I stood outside last week beneath the brightest full moon in 133 years, one week before the new millennium, and I tried my best to care.

It is not easy, being human and trying to know what to make of these momentous mileposts as they go sputtering by.

It made me feel small, standing there beneath the moon and the rest of the universe, so pretty soon I shrank and was a kid again.

A kid again – born in the '50s, growing up in the '60s, a product of American culture if ever there was one. The year 2000 seemed so far away, so impenetrable and mysterious, so hard to contemplate. The year 2000 was like the dark side of the moon.

When I was 12 or 13, I could do subtraction in my head, so I knew that I would be 45 years old when the year 2000 came. But it was a useless piece of information – a story with no pictures and no words.

First of all, it just didn't seem plausible that I would ever make it to 45 years old.

My world raced along on the tilting edge of calamity. I fell out of trees. I slid head-first into second base. I jumped off rock jetties into the churning ocean. I crashed my bike. I crashed my skateboard. I crashed my face against my brother's fist.

My knees were always skinned, or my elbow bruised or my toe stubbed. I broke two skinny ribs, a nose and a wrist. I broke other people's windows, vases and plates. And other people, well, sometimes they broke my heart.

If indeed I did make it to the Year 2000, would it be like "The Jetsons" on TV? Would it be like "Lost in Space," or like Tomorrowland at Disneyland? Or maybe it would be like the Watts riots. Maybe the Vietnam War would still be going on. Maybe they would still be killing the presidents and the Martin Luther Kings and the other heroes.

Would there be anything left at all? I wondered – crouched beneath a school desk, practicing how to duck and cover during a nuclear attack — how big a pile of dust would I make?

Mostly I wondered about my family. Would Mom and Dad live that long? My brother and sister? What about Grandma and Grandpa? What would the world be like without Grandma's enchiladas and Grandpa's jokes?

What about my dog, Barney? In the year 2000, he'd be about 280 in dog years. Surely, though, he would be there. He was always there.

And would I ever have a family of my own? How on earth would I do that? I wouldn't be able to model it after my parents' shattered marriage, that's for sure. But maybe I could model it after Grandma and Grandpa, who were on their way to 60 years of matrimony.

How would I ever find a bride? What girl would have a skinny guy with skinned knees and a knack for breaking plates? Not Sheila Britt. Not Patty Garagiulo. Not Gail Seidman. By 13, they'd already turned me down.

The '60s went on, and the hemlines went up to thigh level, and then back down to the ankles, and a generation turned away from baseball to dream of a better humanity. A world of peace, harmony and earth people all seeking higher consciousness. It was, after all, the dawning of the Age of Aquarius.

Who could have known, after that golden dawn, that by hazy mid-afternoon we'd wind up going through the disco '70s, the go-go '80s and the gizmo '90s?

I didn't know it. I barely noticed any of the big stuff. As I said, I am not good at noticing momentous mileposts as they go sputtering by.

I see only the little ones, too small for the rest of the planet to notice.

Barney was the first to go, run over by the milk truck. Then Grandpa got a tumor in his stomach from worrying about Grandma, and in a week he was gone. Then Grandma, missing Grandpa, slowly followed. Then Dad went, without ever having made up with Mom.

The rest of us, we're still here. We're left gazing up at the fullest moon in 133 years and thinking to ourselves, "Gee, I've seen brighter moons than this."

And so I wander back into the house, with the nagging sense that if Jesus were being born in the next manger over, I'd probably be too busy to notice, scrubbing down the jackass.

The full moon bounces my reflection off the glass in the front door. That ain't no 12- or 13-year-old looking back at me.

I did not expect this thick waist line. I did not expect these nose hairs. I did not expect my skinned elbows to ever heal over. But unexpected things happen in 45 years.

A bride did take me in, for instance, and together we had children of our own. They're 12 and 13, too, just like I was once – just minutes ago, it seems.

I go inside the house to wake them all up. There's a full moon out here that I want them to see.

Maybe they'll know what to make of it.

My Latent Horticultural Tendencies

When he retired from baseball last year, the great Philadelphia Phillies slugger Mike Schmidt admitted he wanted to stay home and grow roses.

I almost picked that moment to come out of the closet and reveal my latent horticultural tendencies.

Here was a man who once hit four home runs in a single game, publicly confessing he was going to retire and grow flowers that have names like Dainty Bess and Angel Face. He wasn't going to hunt, fish or become a mercenary soldier. He was growing roses.

I waited for the sports columnists to pounce on Schmidt's revelation as if he'd just had a sex-change operation. But they didn't. They ignored those roses in the same way that the House of Hanover ignored the chance that Jack the Ripper was of royal blood.

Just the same, I didn't choose that moment to admit to my old cronies that lately I too have felt this strange urge to garden. I didn't want old friends to stop inviting me to ballgames, fishing trips or mercenary outings. I figured I'd wait until this spring.

Then this spring an item in The New York Times told of how Wall Street wheeler-dealers are bailing out to become gardeners.

"Horticulture schools throughout the country are seeing a steady increase in adults who are thinking of leaving their careers to dig in the dirt for a living," the Times reported. "It is not embarrassing these days to leave Wall Street for a career in gardening."

Great. I'm just about to announce I'm a gardener, and all of a sudden every yuppie in the nation is a gardener too. They're buying $40 pruning shears, $100 shovels and $1,000 teak benches. They'll soon drive the prices so high I won't be able to afford manure.

A couple of things are causing all this. First is job stress. One 39-year-old foreign exchange trader who's now hoping to buy a small landscape company explained that the garden is his refuge from a job where "I hear my pulse in my ears."

I'll admit there are days when I can see my pulse in my fingernails.

A second factor is what marketing types identify as "cocooning," in which people begin staying close to home – probably because their mortgages are so high they can't afford to go out. And a third is simple: age.

I'll be turning 36 this month. If you had told me 10 years ago that in a decade I'd be spending Saturday afternoons constructing terraced gardens for delphiniums and hollyhocks, I'd have splurted Scotch whisky across your chest.

I'm not sure when the symptoms began. It had something to do with the sudden convergence of four significant events: One, I took a job in management; two, I had kids; three, I bought a house; and four, I got a vasectomy.

The first event introduced me to a whole new world of workaday responsibilities. Then, having kids introduced a whole new level of vulnerability. Buying a house introduced a whole new breed of debt. And then the vasectomy caused my prefrontal lobes to start eroding – something you don't hear about, because only vasectomized men know it happens and they conspire not to tell you since misery loves company.

Instead of telling you about the erosion of their prefrontal lobes, vasectomized men tell you it won't hurt a bit. And then they grow pansies.

The syndrome began when I built an elaborate fence around the steep boundaries of my new house to keep the kids in and the world out. The fence looked bare. It needed a vine. But vines wouldn't grow because all the topsoil had been scraped away by contractors. So I began building beds of soil. And soon I was learning to build retaining walls and lay bricks and cut hillside terraces that would have made Incas see spots.

For three years I built garden structures more for their therapeutic value than for their aesthetic value. I became quite good at building these monuments to stress. But eventually, as I ran out of space to build new things, I came to the inescapable conclusion that I would need to start growing plants to civilize all the new territory these structures had provided me.

I entered a whole new world of seed catalogs and garden stores. There I would see others of my ilk, slipping in quietly, wearing sunglasses lest somebody they knew drove by. We'd stare curiously at rhododendrons and flats of ground cover. We'd read the fine print on sprinkling systems and roach traps. We'd ask elderly women for advice on aphids. We'd pass our hands contemplatively through mulch and chicken poop.

At first, my plants grew slowly. I'd put in plenty of manure, but there'd be too much shade. I'd get the shade right, but forget to test the pH factor. I'd get the pH right but some newfangled worm would come along and have larkspur pie.

Then, gradually, it began to come together. A small herbaceous border actually bloomed. A clematis vine fought its way up the fence. And when climbing roses inched over the top of an English trellis and swelled with hundreds of buds, I felt as if I'd just driven a Dave Stewart forkball into the centerfield bleachers.

Well, sort of.

Gradually, the file cabinets near the window in my upstairs study have become handy places to put seedling pots. I find myself blaring Rickie Lee Jones through the stereo into the garden when I work because I figure the poppies will prefer it to Springsteen.

"For crying out loud, what is with you?" my wife asks, her eyeballs doing backflips.

I rise at dawn now, slip into scruffy clothes and start my days in the garden. I feed plants, prune them, and I hunt down slugs with the fervor of Zulu teenagers at a fertility dance. The dew makes things glisten, and the silence makes me listen to sounds that I'd forgotten about during the last screeching decade.

By the time I leave for work in the morning, I feel balanced and recharged.

Unfortunately, my hobby was discovered simultaneously by yuppies who have pushed sales at garden centers nationwide to $5.4 billion in 1987 from $2.9 billion in 1982, twice as fast as other retail growth.

So instead of merely admitting to old friends that I've got latent horticultural tendencies, coming out of the closet means they might also call me a yuppie.

Guess I'll just keep my mouth shut.

Call Me "Man Who Runs With Elk"

I am running as fast as I can across the top of a hill and straight toward the sea. I am running with a herd of wild elk.

On my left, not more than 30 yards away, the tule elk stampede. They run fluidly together, these huge animals, with their hooves clacking like water over stones in a big rumbling river.

Fifty more yards and we shall run across the crest of a ridge, side by side in full stride. And my children will look up from the trail far below, and they won't believe their eyes. It will be one of the defining visions of their childhood. They will look up and see their father come over the ridgetop, with a wild look in his eye, running alongside a thundering herd of elk.

And my wife, she'll look up and think – well, who knows what the heck she'll think.

I don't know what comes over me.

It was one of those magnificent autumn days at Point Reyes. We had gone hiking on Tomales Point Trail. A mile out on the trail we saw the herd. It was grazing in an arroyo about 500 yards off to the east. We struck out across the chaparral, where two or three other sets of hikers had settled in to watch.

We got to within about 75 yards and sat down. Soon the girls were creeping nearer to the elk herd, drawn in by the magnetism of more than 100 large animals.

The female elk were calling, and the girls began to imitate the call. "I hope I didn't just say, 'Will you marry me,' " one of them quipped.

Sure enough, within a few minutes one of the herd's three great bulls noticed us. Like a huge sheepdog with antlers, he circled his herd and shuttled them to a safer distance, up the side of the arroyo.

A couple of the other hikers moved closer, and soon the elk were running. In three great, synchronized movements, they rumbled up the far side of the arroyo and over a distant ridge.

The show was over. We walked back to the trail, thinking perhaps we would see them again on our way back.

A few hundred yards back along the main trail, I plunged off to find the elk again. My family opted not to follow, leaving me free to chase the herd alone.

I strode excitedly, trotting across the hills, sensing that the herd would be just over the next ridge.

And soon, there they were, grazing obliviously.

I don't know what comes over me.

Once at Tahoe I was on the porch of a cabin with some friends when we saw a brown bear lumbering down the road. I jumped up without thinking. Not until I had followed the bear into the woods did I realize nobody had come with me. But I couldn't stop. The bear finally caught my scent and turned to stare at me from 25 yards. Scared, I backed away. But I felt so alive.

Another time in the desert I had a similar experience with wild burros. And I regularly paddle a surfboard in the "red triangle" where great white sharks breed.

It's not a death wish, this compulsion to dangle my toes in the food chain. It's a life wish.

Now I approach the elk herd all alone. Free to be foolish, I stalk like a Miwok. Every corpuscle is tuned in. Something primal moves within me.

Suddenly the wind turns and gives away my scent. The elk stop grazing and their heads pop up, one after another, to stare at me.

And then, well – I don't know what comes over me – I begin to trot straight at the herd.

For a moment they just stare at me, as if they can't believe their eyes. This idiot is running straight at them. Obviously he has let his Sierra Club membership lapse.

Then they begin to run. No, not run – stampede. They begin to stampede to the west. About 30 yards away from them now, I veer and run in the same direction.

My heart is thumping to the beat of what would be a very lively fiddle tune if there were anyone here to play. But there is nobody here – only me, running silently as hard as I can alongside a herd of charging elk.

That's when I have the notion: If I can just keep up for a little bit farther, we will come thundering across the top of that ridge. And down below, my wife and kids will look up. This sight will be emblazoned across their memories. When I am an old man in my bathrobe gasping for breath, they will look at me and remember that once upon a time, I ran with the elk.

Except that now I become aware of a new turn of events. Three bull elk in full stride have now moved to the herd's outer flank, closest to me. Their nostrils are flaring and their eyeballs are bulging – and it's me they're looking at. And sure enough, they are steering the herd toward … toward me!

By the time we hit the ridge, our paths will merge.

Bravado becomes panic as quick as you can say Edward Abbey. I make a 90-degree turn north. Now I am running as fast as I can in the opposite direction. With a jackhammering pulse, I bound over gopher holes and bushes as if there are wings on my feet.

A hundred yards and I slow down just enough to crane my head backward. Phew! They have stopped running and are once again grazing calmly. Ho hum, the elk seem to say. Just another day in the herd. Just another bozo, going native on us.

Ten minutes later, puffing like a typhoon, I catch up to my family. And the thing is, they don't believe a word of it.

A Sentimental Journey on Old I-5

I am driving southbound. It's late afternoon on Interstate 5. The valley is everywhere I look – long, low and ugly. My Toyota's been floored for an hour now. But I'm still being passed by wealthier travelers. A fitting metaphor, I guess, as I head to my 25th high school class reunion. I'll no doubt pull into the parking lot and see all these BMWs that have been passing me.

Twenty-five years? You're jivin' me. How can that be?

Hey, I'm not doing so bad. Got a pretty wife, kids, a job. Still have my hair – several in fact. And I still have a surfboard strapped to the roof of my car, for crying out loud – not to mention this pimple breaking out on my chin.

I've never been to a reunion before. Will I even recognize anyone? Will they recognize me? Do I want them to?

It seems like only yesterday that I was driving as fast as I could northbound. I remember a box of records flew out of my '67 Chevy, somewhere over the Grapevine. I didn't even stop to pick them up.

I was getting the hell out of Orange County, all those years ago. Away from the smog and the sprawl and all the people. And away from the troubles that seemed to follow me around like dung beetles follow a cow.

Cows – geez, this valley stinks. How can anybody live out here in the I-5 wasteland? I've got to roll up my window, even though the older I get, the more I crave fresh air.

Back in high school, I was already craving fresh air. There was never enough of it in the classrooms. There was always a lot of it on the beach.

Will these people even remember me? I'm not sure I was in class enough for them to have seen me. In my junior year, I showed up mainly for the tests, when there wasn't any surf. It was a good thing I tested well.

If they do remember me, will they expect me to be the same person I was? I'm not the same person, you know. I've changed in ways I couldn't begin to count. I've had so many experiences – triumphs and defeats, joys and sorrows. And all of those dreams – why, think of all the naps I've needed, just to accommodate all those dreams.

Will they expect me to act the same way I acted back in high school? Worse still, when I get around them, will I indeed begin to act that way?

Interstate 5. This is the part of the state they never put in the tourist brochures. I stop for gas somewhere between Los Banos and Lost Hemorrhoid.

I pull out a tape of oldies. Crank it up for "All Along the Watchtower." Play a little air guitar on the steering wheel. Try not to swerve under the 18-wheeler. Oh, here's the Animals. "When I was young it was more important/ Pain more painful, laugh so much louder, yeah. ..."

Yeah, when I was young. The song reminds me of a road trip to Jalama with Freck and Pete. Must have been 1969.

I wonder whatever happened to Freck and Pete?

And why was it that Freck and Pete always got away with everything? The rest of us would get busted for every impolite little transgression, while Freck and Pete would waltz along feloniously, breaking all the rules and getting away clean.

Ha! Bet they're in Sing Sing by now.

Vesty, Tatkin and Blakeman were on those Jalama trips, too. Surely they'll be at this reunion – pulling up in BMWs. Vesty's probably a dentist now, like his dad. Tatkin had an architecture scholarship at Berkeley, last I saw of him, and he needed to borrow 10 bucks,

which he is going to have to pay back if he shows up. And Blakeman –
slightly psychotic Blakeman.

Well, maybe Blake's in prison with Freck and Pete. I remember
too well the gleam in his eye as he whipped out a Bowie knife in Big
Sur and carved a tick's head out of my arm.

Big Sur's probably right over there, west of those ugly hills. Whose
idea was I-5, anyway?

I wonder what happened to the Kissinger kids? Bubbling Kurt,
who lost the car keys while defecating in the woods on a surf trip
somewhere near San Onofre. And sister Taina – what a cutie she was,
strumming Joni Mitchell songs on her guitar at Maureen's house.

Ah, Maureen's house. I cannot think of her mischievous, straight-
A's-without-trying smile without grinning myself. She got it from her
dad, who used to love to gather us teens at his dinner table, sip Chivas
and hold forth on the great books we must read. He called me the
King of the One Liners. One line was all I could get in edgewise.

There at the table would be Mo, Chris, Mary Sue and Esther of
the strawberry hair. Esther played sad songs on the piano the week
before we graduated.

I guess I'd like to see some of those people after all. Maybe I'll be
able to explain why I never said goodbye.

Except to Mindy. I did my damnedest to say goodbye to her. She
didn't really want to hear it, though – she just wanted me gone. She
just sorta demolished my aorta, as the country singers on I-5 radio
might say. Took one big, first-love karate chop at my mojo.

Ah, Mindy. I'm sure she doesn't look like she looked back then in
a summer breeze and a cotton dress. Someone told me she had grown
a soft belly and a hard edge. I think I saw the beginnings of the hard
edge one night in '73 when she thought I'd betrayed her with a girl
named Dana. Within weeks, she had carved my left ventricle into filets
and cast me off like chum.

She probably doesn't even remember.

Here's the Grapevine. I'd better speed up around this convoy of
big rigs.

When I get down there, I'll put in a token appearance at the
reunion. Then I'll turn around and go to the ocean, where there's plenty of air – just the way I always used to.

Sleepwalking, Hand in Hand With My Father

Us newspaper hacks are creatures of habit. We're just factory workers in the Information Age. We get used to things being a certain way. Our concentration depends on it. If things get moved around, our concentration goes out the window.

It's human nature, I guess. When things change suddenly, we stagger, we lose our bearings, we get a little numb. And then we go on functioning, doing what we've been trained to do, falling back on the safety net of our own experience.

Consider the paragraphs I started to write last week as a column. It was shortly after The Business Journal had finished weeks of office remodeling. The place had been crawling with construction workers. When we finally settled into our new configuration, I sat furtively at my spanking new work station, in my own little cubicle, and tried to write. Here's how it went. . .

This is the first sentence I have written since I moved my desk.

How was it? Was my first sentence all right? I'm not sure, because I'm not used to looking north at my sentences. I'm used to looking west when I write them.

Oh, I'll get used to it. I've written sentences while looking north before …

At that moment, just as I had finished those words, the phone rang at my work station.

It was my brother, and I knew immediately from his voice that things had changed forever in our lives.

"Dad died this morning," he said.

The rest of the conversation, I don't remember.

I have often heard the expression that people "go numb" when they receive terrible news. Until that moment, I assumed the expression was a metaphor – that people go numb emotionally. I did not understand that the expression had anything to do with a physical condition.

I had to get out of the office, so I went walking. And long before any tears came, the skin on my face, my hands, my arms – it all literally went numb. For several hours, I could not seem to feel it.

Nor could I corner my thoughts. I stayed at work, trying to focus on what had to be done. When my friend called to confirm our usual Tuesday afternoon racquetball game, I offered to drive.

I didn't mention it – I didn't know how. We began to play. I felt unusually graceful and powerful, and I had none of my normal shortage of wind. I felt, strangely, as if my father was watching – just like when he would come to my Little League games.

The first game was hard-fought, with long rallies, lots of running. As usual, my friend won. As we started our second game, I seemed to feel stronger instead of weaker. I guess you don't feel winded when you are numb.

The second game was incredible. Endless rallies. I was chasing down every shot, hitting miraculous returns. Suddenly, the game was over and I had won.

I sat down on the floor of the court, and a silly, corny thought floated through my head. I'm glad I won that one, I thought to myself, with Dad watching.

And that was it. The protective coating of numbness was gone. I was choking back sobs and trying to explain to my friend. He looked aghast. How could I have played racquetball on the day that my father died?

"That's a big one, Lee – that's about as big as they get, " he said. "You can't hold it in."

But now wasn't the time. The sobs stopped. We talked. And then I went back to work.

Like I said, when our world changes on us, we become disoriented. And then our instincts take over as a safety net, we go on functioning.

It's a little bit somnambulistic, as if we are sleepwalking.

For 10 years I had been bracing myself to lose Dad. His health had been failing him, one thing at a time. But he had hung in there. A massive aneurysm, and he hung in there. Leg amputated for diabetes, and he hung in there. More surgeries, toes removed – he hung in there. He was tough, a longshoreman all his life. I talked to him a couple of weeks ago, and he was going out to buy a new pair of cowboy boots.

I tried to brace myself by grappling with my own perceptions of my father. As a father, you couldn't call him a raging success. He was my hero, but he wasn't there enough. He missed a lot of child support payments. As I grew up, I grew bitter. There were 10 years there when I never saw or spoke to him.

It was my wedding day when we finally spoke. There was a catch in his voice, there was a catch in mine. And we spent the next 10 years trying to level with each other. Somehow, we had to tell each other things we could not even put into words.

When they took off his leg four years ago, I thought I was going to lose him. I drove all night, knowing the words, mouthing the words. But when I got there they had him adrift on morphine. I sat heartbroken in the corner.

And then his friends began to arrive. From all over the West they came. Their affection was deep. They were the longshoremen he had worked with, had gone on bloody dock strikes with, had drunk and gambled with on the graveyard shift. They were the men who had leaned on each other, in their own ways, when their own fathers had died.

I watched them talk all night long about my dad, about the old days, laughing as he lay there half-conscious.

For the first time, I began to see my dad, not as the father we both wished he could have been, but as a man like me.

And the need for blame was replaced by a need for forgiveness.

The last time we talked, we veered from those new cowboy boots he wanted for his one leg. We talked about his own childhood. And the need for forgiveness was replaced by a sense of understanding. The last thing he said before we hung up the phone was "I love you, son."

Love is a moving target. Life is a moving target.

I'm leaving now to see him one last time. The numbness wears off again, like morphine, and another wave hits.

A Pair of New Year's Day Soliloquies

Almost New Year's Day, 1980. I sit in the slim but welcome shade of a screwbean mesquite tree. We're on the floor of a high-desert valley, the tree and I, marking the passage of time by counting the number of times a hawk must flap its wings to escape our view.

Screwbean mesquite. I like that name. It has a conspiratorial ring to it. The tree keeps me cool in the midday heat, and I spill an occasional warm beer near its thirsty roots. We're pals.

The rest of the Northern Hemisphere is frozen up tighter than an Eskimo's grin, but out here it's 85 degrees. My camp is spartan. There are hot springs, a couple of palm trees and a few other loners who've driven four hours of nut-jarring dirt roads to be here – roads full of rocks that were taught at an early age to leap high and do bad things to the undercarriages of cars.

There are no civilized amenities, save those we've brought. I've been here a week. My feet are propped up on an ice chest that's getting alarmingly light to heft. I wear only an old pair of Navajo moccasins, a rat-gnawed tomato picker's hat and some shorts that were obsolete long ago.

Screwbean mesquite. Heh-heh. It's named after the curly shape of its seed.

Out here the mind can travel as fast and fleet afoot as a whiptail lizard. But like the lizard, the mind scurries only when provoked. This is particularly true at high noon. The mind is not, after all, stupid.

For New Year's, I try to think about where I've been for the last decade and where the new decade will take me. I own nothing and nothing owns me; the potential is enormous. But my mind is not up to provocation today. So it drifts, further and further ...

... A cloud of white alkaline dust rises like a smoke signal across the valley floor. It arrives to a chorus of harps and bells – the bus from Lonely Mountain All Girls Conservatory. It is loaded with squealing young women on a field trip, and some of them want me to show them around ....

A branch of remembering mesquite spears my cheek, and I crack an eye from my daydream to see that there is no bus. Only the sun, loafing west toward the Inyo Mountains. Shadows form, bringing new shape and color to this rugged place. It is time to walk.

Across the valley – I cannot gauge its distance, for the air is too clear and there are no manmade landmarks – a volcanic cinder cone rises red and Paleozoic from the desert floor. That's where I'll go.

Out hiking, the desert is not flat and barren as it appears from a distance. It is gullied and textured by flash floods and wind, teeming with obstinate life that's intricate in its simplicity. Hardy creosote bushes, sunbleached sandstone sprinkled with chert and obsidian. I scramble into, across and out of gullies separated by broad plateaus. It is hot, but my sweat is dried quickly by a warm wind and I'm just cool enough. The cadence of my moccasins piercing alkaline soil is all I hear – a sound Paiutes would know.

In a gully, the earth starts to shake. I scramble up the other side just in time to let a pack of wild burros charge past, nostrils flaring, unshod hooves beating furiously as they run – from what?

I keep hiking toward the cinder cone, fooled by distance that is distorted in rippling hot air. In a labyrinth of stone, the remains of an old Indian hogan offer a shady place to pause. I shoo out a scorpion and crouch inside, but it is not restful. Someone was here once, encamped perhaps in the shade of screwbean mesquite. I stare until there are shaman faces in the shadows of rocks. Then, spooked like a sparrow in a cave of bats, I walk on. All my senses are kindled now.

Somewhere I once read that Indians used to make clicking noises when they walked in the desert if they wanted to alert rattlesnakes to their presence. As I reach a shattered field of burnt sienna rocks near the foot of the cinder cone and begin to climb, my mouth clicks faster than the shuffling of a deck of cards.

Up and up I climb. The giddying sky is broad, and the desert is vibrating now in hues. Colors simmer and melt, shimmer and bend as the day cools down.

A pair of hawks circles above me, drifting slowly on waves of air. Climbing, I am soon beside them. And at last, as I make the last push to the top of the cinder cone – which is far higher than I thought – the hawks are below me.

I have never looked down at hawks in flight before. I can see their corded muscles flexing to meet constantly changing drafts. They subtly adjust their wings and float skyward, heads craned down in their search for the game that frees them to survive.

Now the hawks are circling me. And now they are above me, spiraling higher and higher into the desert sky.

I don't know how long I stand on the mountaintop watching the hawks disappear before I realize that my arms are fully outstretched and I am laughing, as if my blood has been replaced by air and I, too, will ascend to grand heights.

Almost New Year's Day, 1990. I sit beneath a low ceiling in the upstairs study of this house that owns me. I mark the passage of time by listening to a vacuum cleaner and kids shouting. It is a comfortable house, but discomforting to feel owned. My feet, shod in practical shoes, are propped up on a desk full of work to be done. Every year, there is more work to be done and less time to do it. Screwbean mesquite does not grow in my garden.

I want to write a story that will question what difference a decade makes. I want to tell of how time passes but cannot erode who you are.

I want to, but the words don't move as fluidly as they used to. I resolve to find time to walk in a desert – but I've been saying that for years now.

Another year passes, another deadline approaches, and another hawk flies away swiftly and unseen.

Our Backward Views on Vacation

There was nobody there but us and the monkeys. I floated on my back in the hot springs. A few feet away, my wife and 14-year-old daughter sat laughing behind a waterfall. Our 12-year-old swung out on a rope beneath the moon and let go.

Suddenly, the clouds parted and there it was – the volcano Arenal, just a mile away, a perfect black cone jutting far up into the night. Rivers of red molten lava streamed from top to bottom, and our jaws dropped.

Paradise in the rain forests of Costa Rica.

Paradise, not because of the volcano or the hot springs. Not because of the ginger-scented air, or the butterflies and flowers and ferns. Not because of the empty, palm-fringed beaches, or the mangoes, or the toucans, or the piña coladas made from angel spit.

None of those things made it paradise. No, it was paradise because my family was there, sharing an adventure.

We Americans are afloat in unparalleled prosperity. But when it comes to taking time off – serious amounts of time, enough for people to recharge and families to regroup – we are still in the Stone Age.

My family is just one example of why time off matters. We needed this trip. We had saved for years to take it. We wound up spending more than we saved. And it was worth every cent. For three weeks, traveling together in a place where we had never been before, we learned to laugh in unison again. We learned to see things again. We learned again that what matters most to us is each other.

We were bonded again at a pivotal time in our lives.

This week, just seven days after returning, Rachel started high school; I dropped her off on Monday morning, wide-eyed and ready for her next step toward independence. Meanwhile, Lauren starts 7th grade next week. She, too, is feeling her oats, a lanky colt who will soon be too tall to sit in my lap and call me Daddy.

They are growing up so fast. And for our little family, the growing pains have been acute.

Children start to act like jerks when they hit adolescence, my wife says, because that's nature's way of making it easier for us to let them go.

Nature can hurt. We knew it was coming, but still it was painful when our kids began to shine us on. When they would rather be with their friends. When they would spend hours on the phone. When they would become annoyed or sullen at our appalling stupidity.

Treating us badly hurt them as much as it did us. But adolescence seemed to have a momentum all its own.

When I decided, rather abruptly, that it was now or never – we were taking a big, three-week trip together, and I had chosen Costa Rica – I met a mix of excitement and revulsion. They wanted to go, but couldn't their friends come? They so feared missing something in their little worlds that they had no appetite for the big world.

We bought guidebooks and made them at least look at the pictures. We took them to REI for mosquito nets and hiking boots. We put them in charge of sunscreen and bug repellent. Bit by bit, the impending adventure began to fire their imaginations. By the day we left, they were psyched. When the plane touched down and we set out on rutted roads across a magnificent country, they were given to fits of giggling.

Still, it took about 10 days in Costa Rica before the more surly vestiges of teenagism had evaporated.

At first, they were worried about what they were missing. Rachel sent her friends 27 post cards in the first five days. They looked anxiously for a TV, but found only Spanish programs. They played tapes in the car of their favorite radio stations back home.

But soon, the taped commercial radio seemed out of place. In a week, they stopped sending post cards to friends and instead addressed their last few to themselves – a sort of journal entry, as if they knew that when they got home they would need pinching to remember they had really seen crocodiles, and caught waves, and ridden horses in the cloud forest, and shot on a cable like Tarzan past two-toed sloths amid the jungle canopy.

They began reading voraciously. And trying to speak Spanish with the people they met. And they sat quietly on the beach painting the horizon in water colors.

As they got beyond their self-obsession, they became sisters again. And even Mom and Dad were cool.

My point is not what we did on our summer vacation. The trip could have been to just about anywhere new. My point is that it's crucially important to take time off, whether it be as a family that needs to regain its footing, or as an individual who must regain passion for life.

And yet, in this country, we're lucky if we get two weeks of paid vacation a year. We feel guilty about taking more, as if we're somehow doing less than our part.

In Western Europe, four to eight weeks are standard in countries where per capita productivity rivals our own. In some places, vacation bonuses – up to 8 percent of salary – are paid to make sure people get away.

According to a national survey of the changing work force, U.S. workers in 1997 were working 3.5 more hours a week than they did 20 years earlier. They work more hours than they are scheduled to work, bring more work home and take more business trips.

We've got to stop feeling guilty about taking vacations, and start feeling guilty about not taking them.

The Primordial Hunter Feeds His Family

My car is beginning to float away.

I am waiting to turn left into a Placerville pizza parlor's parking lot in the first big rainstorm of the year. What might very well pass for a river is thundering down at me from an intersecting street. And now my damned car is beginning to float. I have no anchor.

This is one mean rainstorm, and it's peaking right about now. In a stroke of idiocy, it has been ordained that I should go out in one mean rainstorm that's peaking right about now to pick up a pizza. For the sake of a pizza, I am going to be swept out to sea in a foreign car – and I don't even have a tape deck. If I did, it would be playing Linda Ronstadt's "Desperate Auto."

This is heck on earth. I drove down here without thinking. I had to have a pizza so bad I did not retreat when I discovered the rain was falling so hard I could not see out of my car – faster than the windshield wipers could wipe it. And the wind – the wind took assertiveness training.

With my senses of sight and sound drowned out by the squall, I drove by intuition. I drove by a primordial hunter's instinct. I drove by sense of smell and taste – I could almost smell and taste that pizza.

Plump tomatoes quivering juicily in seductive satin sheets of cheese ...

The rain beat on my car like a thousand Zulu drummers whacking out a tune at a fertility dance. At one point, I hit a puddle so deep my car hydroplaned and shot sideways, the steering wheel jerking like a halibut in my hands. But I plunged on in hunger.

Bellpeppers doing the tango with shapely mushrooms ...

I got down to the boulevard and it looked like the street had been nuked. Not a creature stirring. The power was out. Gas stations were still. Streetlights had packed it in and gone to Mexico for winter. I didn't care. I'd row if I must. Pizza – I must have pizza!

Steamy onions doing the rumba in an oregano mist ...

My itinerary called for me to stop for a six-pack, but I couldn't find the liquor store. Oh, it was probably there, all right, stocked with booze and Beer Nuts and Twinkies that nobody could buy because the lights were out and you couldn't see the store. I resolved to pay exorbitant prices for a six-pack at the pizza parlor ... if I could find the pizza parlor!

A wave of panic broke over me. What if I couldn't find the pizza parlor? (Gasp.) What if the pizza parlor's power is out too, and its ovens are all-electric? (Moan.)

Hot anchovies doing the cha-cha on a divine dance floor of dough ...

A long stream of headlights poured toward me at the intersection where I must turn left. I braked to a gentle stop. I waited.

And now, suddenly, my stomach does a double take.

What? I don't – there! It did it again! Am I getting ill? Am I spinning into pizza vertigo? I – there! It did it again!

My car is floating. Geez. Just what I need.

A hopeful thought drips into my fevered brain: Perhaps the river coming down Carson Road will sweep me toward the pizza parlor! But no – no luck. I begin to float back toward the car behind me. Whoa! This is getting serious. It's time to get a grip. Time for heroism. E pizzabus unum – in pizza we trust.

A break in traffic. I slam the car into first gear and let 'er rip. My tires spin, uselessly at first. Luckily, they have a snow tread. It creates a paddlewheel effect. I begin to move and – suddenly! - the wheels touch pavement. My car raises on its haunches in triumph! I careen into the parking lot.

Piz-za! Piz-za! Piz-za!

Pendulous pepperoni mambos wantonly in silky mozzarella ...

I fight hard against the wind and manage to open my car door. I
wade across the flood, bravely leaning into the heart of the monsoon
beast. It seems an eternity, but I plod on. At last I waddle through the
door and into the fragrant sanctuary of the pizza shrine.

Thank God for auxiliary sources of electricity! The pizza parlor's
ovens have not malfunctioned!

I slide up to the counter, feeling weathered and rough like Bogey in
"Treasure of the Sierra Madre" and mutter, "Wessman – large combo to
go." Quickly, currency is traded and the deal is done. The pizza is mine!

Again I button up my Eskimoesque parka. I suck in a deep
breath, snort once or twice in defiance, and dash outside.

Oh wow. Heck on earth again.

All the way home, intoxicated by the fumes wafting nostrilward
from the passenger seat, I fight against the rogue storm. I drive with
my forehead jammed against the windshield, peering hard, trying to
see where the road is going next, struggling valiantly against the nervous tension that ties my stomach in knots and threatens to render useless my pizza-digesting mechanisms.

Somehow – oh merciful, benevolent luck! - I make it back to the
house. Holding my precious bounty snug against my throbbing bosom
to shield it from the rain, I crouch and run like Eric Dickerson –
crushing hapless raindrops in my path – through the gate, across the
yard, through a pile of dog doo and into the candle-lit living room.
(The power is out here, too.)

My eyeballs are bulging like Peter Lorre's. I don't wait for plates to
be fetched from the kitchen. No! I shriek. Now! Me want pizza NOW!

Like an enraged caveman, I shred the box and foil that encases my
prey. With bare hands I tear off a chunk. With a grunt of passionate,
furious victory, I stuff a wad of it into my mouth.

The pizza is cold. I was afraid of that.

Precious Time and the Element of Choice

We climbed up the calvary hall to Steve Wilford's room, unready for the crucifixion on the other side of the door.

Our friend lay dying.

Acquired immune deficiency syndrome had ravaged Steve's body swiftly and cruelly. One of the most gifted people I've known was losing the simple gift of living through his 39th year.

He was sleeping feverishly. Friends, knowing they might not get to see him again, had begun to gather in his South Land Park home. Nobody knew quite what to say. Words were feeble in the face of this. We mustered into small groups and went back to see Steve.

Most of us came back out of the room alone.

It stunned me that I barely recognized him at first. Despite meticulous care, he was emaciated. He lay in dappled light, covered to the waist in a white sheet. His thick hair was swept back by a damp washcloth. I wanted to keep a cheerful face, but tears welled up and I fought visions of nails in his palms.

There will be half a million AIDS cases by 1991, federal officials tell us. In California, 7,000 have already died, and 50,000 will be stricken within three years. I've shuddered at the numbers, just like you. But this wasn't a number.

For a minute or two, I stood beside Steve's bed while he slept. Suddenly, his eyes opened wide with a start and drove directly into mine. A second passed slowly. And then a big smile of recognition crossed his lips. He tried to speak but could not form words. Neither could I.

"You've grown a beard," I stammered, "since the last time I saw you."

That had been at lunch nine weeks earlier. He still looked strong, then, although 18 months of experimental AIDS remedies and a bout with pneumosistis had grayed and weakened him.

We ate at Juleps. He was just leaving his job as No. 2 guy at the state Board of Medical Quality Assurance. He had written a splendid series of articles for The Business Journal on dealing with AIDS in the workplace, and we had just syndicated the articles to about 30 newspapers nationally.

He had other irons in the fire, too. He was weighing offers from publishers on a mystery he had co-authored, drawing from the days when he worked for a private detective in San Francisco. And he was getting ready for a trip to New York to see some friends and take in some theater. He was to leave this month.

In retrospect, he seemed to be telling me this might be his last trip, but I didn't really believe that. He looked too strong. And besides, there are some things you just don't want to believe.

What really struck me about that conversation was the way Steve kept turning it back to me. We talked about dying, and what he had gone through to prepare himself and his loved ones. I could not imagine maintaining such dignity in the face of so much anguish. But he kept turning it back to me – to the problems I was having in life, and the way I was approaching them.

Dying slowly had taught Steve essential truths, and he wanted desperately to share them. They revolved around the preciousness of time and the element of choice. I went home that day and pulled my children close to me and held them until they wriggled away.

A few weeks after our lunch, Steve was back at Sutter General. Lung infections had spread and now doctors took his spleen and part of his liver.

Still, he came through. He hadn't given up on New York, and had even added Jamaica in autumn to his itinerary. He came home, but then, about three weeks ago, he became consumed by fever and began to fight dementia. In a moment of clear thought, he said he wanted to die at home.

And now, on a Sunday afternoon, his friends kept arriving. The care the closest of them had given him was impeccable and courageous. I wondered how many AIDS victims must die without such attention, made pariahs by the intolerant and fearful.

Two of his favorite musicians, Danny Carnahan and Robin Petrie, came from San Francisco to play at the foot of his bed. Everyone else settled back to listen.

I looked around at their faces. For the gay men, there was a tiredness about the eyes. This scene was too familiar, and perhaps too precursive. But tragedy by rote does not diminish the weight of tragedy, and they grieved.

The rest of us looked bewildered and overwhelmed. For most, Steve was our first friend to be felled this way.

Danny and Robin played and I saw Steve dancing on the streets of Edinburgh, Scotland, five years ago.

The four of us had met as part of an amateur theater troupe that wound up taking "Spoon River Anthology," a play we believed in, to the international drama festival there. We had gone on a whim, really, raising just enough money to take 15 people. No American amateur group had ever done it before.

When we arrived, we found ourselves among 600 other productions, with no money left to promote our play. The only way we could attract audiences was to go out every day and busk, performing songs and bits of the show on the sidewalks of Edinburgh, then making sales pitches that would have done P.T. Barnum proud. We had come a long way and this was arduous. When we hit rock bottom, it was largely Steve's energy that buoyed us. He danced hardest on the street. And by the end of those three weeks, Cinderella appeared; the show won critical acclaim and packed houses, and we went home in a gilded pumpkin. It was a precious time.

I'll always think of Steve dancing on The High Street at Parliament Square. But I'll also have to recall him dying of an insidious virus, long before his rightful time.

While Danny and Robin were still playing to him, I left quietly.

It was late when I got home. I pulled out a scrapbook and came across one of Steve's lines from "Spoon River": "Passer-by, sin beyond any sin is the sin of blindness of souls to other souls. And joy beyond any joy is the joy of having the good in you seen, and seeing the good at the miraculous moment."

Steve slipped away a week later.

Hank and Dave
Dance with Alligators

In "Peter Pan," that classic of modern literature, time is portrayed as an angry crocodile. With an alarm clock in its belly, it relentlessly pursues that vile antagonist of Peter Pan and all things young and carefree, Captain Hook.

(When you have small children, you start finding your literary metaphors in weird places.)

Anyway, this all comes to mind because of last weekend's 40th birthday party for Hank and Dave.

Turning 40 is not an easy thing to do, psychologically speaking. It's a milestone that tends to be worn about the neck. If you're not careful, it can cause your shoulders to stoop and your knees to weaken.

Dozens of us gathered in a rented bungalow last weekend to act the part of the crocodile for these two boyhood buddies, Hank and Dave.

No, on second thought, strike that crocodile and make it an alligator – we acted the part of alligators.

And that, I think, is why Hank and Dave were able to turn 40 more gracefully, more soulfully, more Peter Panfully, than most people turn 40.

Maybe I'd better explain.

There's this dance called The Alligator, see. And for the last seven years or so, ever since I missed Hank's wedding, I've been hearing about this dance called The Alligator. Hank and Dave and some of their friends, led by The Amazing Lance, had gotten really wild at that wedding and had done The Alligator, which they knew from their college days.

Performing The Alligator, as it had been explained to me by its chief proponent, The Amazing Lance, involves casting oneself prone upon the dance floor and crawling about, sort of in rhythm, quite possibly biting women on the ankles. My understanding was that it is best performed to old Motown hits, or maybe Junior Walker and the Allstars.

I'd been trying to get these guys to perform The Alligator in my presence for years, but the stars had never aligned to allow it. These guys were in their 30s, and too old to do The Alligator anymore.

Saturday night, though, they were turning 40 – it was a surprise party designed to either celebrate or mourn the fact – and conditions were right.

Something had to happen. The place was crammed with grown-ups. They talked smally, nodded knowingly, chewed politely on hors d'oeuvres.

Hank and Dave, the birthday boys, acted appropriately 40. They arrived, expressed surprise and then mingled. Correctly. Both, you see, are successful men, family men, adept in their fields. They have behaved themselves, and on this night they seemed aware of the obligation to continue doing so. They danced self-consciously with wives, mothers and daughters. They joked conservatively with business associates and in-laws.

All the while, just beneath the surface, an amphibious current stirred in them. They privately wrestled with this whole turning-40 thing. Their brows occasionally took on new furrows, as if they were trying to make some momentous decision – or else their shoes were too tight. Clearly, they were bothered by something, as men turning 40 often are.

Fortunately, as Hank and Dave dealt with the social discomfort of turning 40, The Amazing Lance, himself 40 or so, conspired back by the bar to rob them of this opportunity to become truly old. He kept glasses full, eyes twinkling, knowing exactly what he was up to. He methodically lured others into his plan.

At one point, he grinned at me, the grin of a conspirator. "I'm feeling reptilian," said The Amazing Lance, legendary alligator dancer.

By 10 p.m. or so, it was time for the obligatory roasting of the birthday boys. A crowd of their old cronies, all turning 40 this year like a string of firecrackers lit by accident, squirmed up to the front of the bungalow and told stories about how wild and crazy they used to be.

The formal act of recalling past glories seemed to be the magic fairy dust they needed. Bit by bit, they began to forget about turning 40, and they all began to think happy thoughts. And, as anyone who has studied Peter Pan knows, fairy dust coupled with happy thoughts causes lost boys to levitate.

By 2 a.m., the music had reached new wattage. The beverages were halfway drained. Most the people who were not yet close to turning 40 or who had long since passed it had left. And those who remained danced with a new fervor, for they had come to understand that this event was not merely a birthday party, but rather, a rite of passage, and if it were not performed according to the protocol of the gods, these men's souls might emerge from their 40th birthdays with hooks instead of left hands.

And suddenly, it happened.

Right in the middle of "Wooly Bully," first Lance, then Hank, then Dave threw themselves violently upon the dance floor. And there, with a passion only they could fathom, they did the Dance Against the Passage of Time – The Alligator.

They did it as they had never done it before. They did it as if they were attacking a school of mermaids. They didn't confine themselves to just crawling on their bellies. They rolled. They somersaulted. They stood on their heads with legs bicycling through the air. They defied gravity. They defied social covenants. They defied time. They went on until dawn and then kept going into the next day.

And so it was that on their 40th birthday, Hank and Dave were exorcised of the worst danger of aging – seriousness.

I am 35. And although I understood what I was seeing, I was too old to throw myself upon the floor. I have not yet reached my moment of truth – that moment when I will have to decide whether I shall go on taking myself as seriously as death, or whether I will let down my pretenses, throw myself down, and dance with alligators and crocodiles.

Traffic School:
a Message From God

So there I was. Guilty, basically. A Highway Patrol plane nabbed me on a long Highway 50 downhill. The hand of justice swooped out of the sky, swift and mighty, and swatted me like a meat bee. The cop said I was doing 70.

So here I am. Bored out of my gourd in traffic offenders' school. Outside, it's a beautiful, sunny Saturday. But in here, beneath fluorescent lights, I sit with 27 other guilty parties. The incessant drone of our instructor's voice is like Chinese water torture as he preaches the Gospel of Defensive Driving. In frustrated unison, we roll our eyes skyward.

Driving school is God's way of saying that you haven't been taking full advantage of your Saturdays.

When you infract the Vehicle Code in this state, if your record isn't too abominable you may be given the option of attending a one-day traffic school to keep the ticket off your record and out of the greedy hands of your insurance company. Many drivers jump at the chance. Verily, they know not at what they jump.

Personally, the tension Friday night before my class is too much. I drink.

My alarm clock explodes Saturday morning. I roll out of bed, flush the clock down the toilet, take a brief nap in the wash basin and head for class.

Milling about outside the classroom are all the other infractors. Many look as if they, too, were tense the night before. Promptly at 7:59 a.m., a righteous-looking fellow marches past us, into the classroom. We follow, instinctively knowing him to be our jailer for a day.

Displaying no visible signs of good humor, John Clark writes his name upon the blackboard, taking care to catch a fingernail, and orders us to drag around all the tables and chairs until they've made a racket quite obscene to those of us who were tense the night before. Then he asks us for $20 apiece. We cough up a total of $560, and for the first time, John Clark smiles.

"This is not a lecture class," he barks. "I want you to listen with open ears." He warns that if we nod off, gab or come in late from a break, he'll expel us. An off-duty probation officer, he is working for a Sacramento company that puts these things on. "I'm here because I'm paid to be here," he crows. And we're here as punishment. That's becoming very clear.

One by one, each of us must say who we are and what we're in for; there are librarians, construction workers, students, a retired teacher, a theater director, real estate agents, tinkers, tailors …

One by one, we confess our crimes. Most of us have alibis. But by the time our confessions trek around the room, we've grown more frank. "I'm a speeding ticket waiting to happen," says one guy. "I drive like a nut," another admits.

This is group therapy for bad drivers.

In our class, 25 were speeding. About half of them were caught by the CHP plane. Nice revenue getter, that plane. George Bush doesn't need a tax hike to control the budget deficit – he just needs a few of those planes.

"If you're lucky, you get a citation and you get to come to traffic school," says Clark. "If you're unlucky, you get in an accident."

One's relative luck, however, is a matter of opinion. By 9:30, a non-crippling accident doesn't sound so bad.

"You should drive as if everybody else on the road is either blind or drunk," we are told.

No wonder our society is so tense and hostile. There are millions of people out there everyday driving defensively. If they all think everybody else is blind or drunk, they must be very peeved. Defensive driving may well be a root cause of our societal ills.

About 9:47, Clark is reciting a barrage of figures about reaction time. My mind drifts off ...

... I remember the time I fell out of the van I was driving. Should've reacted quicker. Shouldn't have been leaning against the door. The van kept going and mowed down a police callbox. I wasn't legally responsible, though, since I wasn't actually driving at the time because I'd fallen –

My daydream is interrupted by the instructor, calling on me to answer a question I didn't hear. "Some of you drivers here are the worst people on the road," he sneers at me like a drill instructor. "You're looking at the same road, the same sign, the same tree every day. Driving becomes automatic. Accidents happen all the time simply because somebody was looking at the scenery ..."

... Yeah. I remember one time I was staring at a woman in a halter top on Main Street and didn't see that old Buick stopped in front of me. It's amazing how much sturdier an old Buick is than a new Toyota. They just don't make 'em like they –

Driftus interruptus. The instructor calls on me again. He looks mad.

At 10:32, he breaks out the first accident photos. Oh, I've been waiting for these. Glad I didn't have breakfast.   .

10:49. Time is moving slower than a snail going up a frozen waterfall. Clark's voice again: "At 35 mph, you lose 25 percent of your peripheral vision. At 45 mph, it's reduced by 35 percent. And at 65 mph, you're reduced to tunnel vision." At the speed this class is going, I've got eyes in the back of my head.

1 p.m. A new topic for discussion: How often should a driver check the rear-view mirror? The answer, Clark says, is every five seconds.

He demonstrates. Holding an imaginary steering wheel, his head swivels in small click-stops from side to side while he counts aloud: "One, two, three, four, five, check! One, two, three, four, five, check! One ..."

1:37. A new topic: How close should you follow another car? Clark explains the three-second rule. He demonstrates. Holding the imaginary wheel. He watches the car ahead of him pass road signs:

"One-thousand one, one-thousand two, one-thousand three. One-thousand one, one-thousand two –

Great. So now, we're driving along, counting the seconds on our mirror checks and following the three-second rule: One, two, three, four, five, check! – one-thousand two, one-thousand three – three, four, five, check! – one-thousand one, one-thousand – two, three, four, check!

We've got a regular little rumba going here. And heaven help us if we try to figure out next week's budget while we're driving. We could wind up with syncopated whiplash. (And bear in mind that everybody else on the road is either blind or drunk.)

2:15. "Don't look at the road right in front of your car; look down the road." I personally am staring at a fly that landed on my booklet 15 minutes ago, right on the "Time Comparison for a 20 Mile Trip" chart.

2:27. A movie on drunk driving. From a critical viewpoint, the film moves slowly and uses cliches to make its point. Besides, it makes me thirsty.

2:54. Topic: Correct positioning of a sun visor. Across the room, the theater director is rehearsing an imaginary scene. The retired teacher is going over a lesson plan she never gave. Three real estate agents are making big sales.

3:11. Clark becomes upset when someone uses the adjective "silly" to describe his procedure for passing a car.

3:55. Movie time again. "Red Asphalt," is the title. Filmed in Plasmacolor. Maybe you've heard of it.

4:30. It is done at last. For having kept our eyes open all day, we each receive certificates, suitable for framing. Some of us weep joyously, some stare blankly. Others vow to have a reunion in 20 years. "I enjoyed having you today," Clark grins, like Dracula.

5:14. I am driving in my car. My seat belt is on. I'm driving more slowly than normal.

Perhaps it's because of the class I've just finished. No. A more likely explanation is that there's no way in the known universe that I ever want to sit through a class like that again.

I'm still having trouble with that rhythm, though, One, two, three, four, five, check! Two-thousand, three-thousand – three, four, five, check!

"Footsyball"

Sharks, Intolerance and Making Life Work

Bigotry: Back to the Drawing Boards

A friend was out jogging. She was on her usual route, out a country road way up in the foothills, out beyond where the houses are, out where the pavement ends and the local teenagers like to make out.

Suddenly she stopped dead in her tracks.

There, scrawled on the tail end of the pavement were swastikas, white-supremacist slogans – the sweet nothings of ancient hatreds, now whispered by our children.

A chill hit her. This familiar road where she always felt safe to jog had in an instant become fearsome. She ran home, wondering about this place where she is bringing up her own teenagers.

The incident got a bunch of us talking. Other recent incidents came out in our conversation:

Like the one at a recent basketball game between rival El Dorado County high schools. The lone black kid on the court had to endure racial epithets from the opposing team, right on the floor in front of a gym full of people. Nobody had been taken to task over the incident. It was allowed to happen.

Or the one where a friend on a local school board met bitter opposition when he tried to persuade his board colleagues to adopt a policy condemning intolerance. "Does that mean we would have to accept homosexuality?" he was asked.

Or the one where a friend on a local affirmative action panel found out that every single black child to attend El Dorado High School in the last 15 years has sustained at least one severe beating at the hands of other students.

And as we talked it became clear that old evils lurk in this place where we live, and nobody seems to want to talk about it.

The local sheriff has started a unit to investigate hate crimes. A small, grassroots "round table" has been formed to discuss issues of intolerance. But there's not a word in the local newspapers, no action by the school boards and damn little notice given by much of anyone.

Down in places like Meadowview and Oak Park, it's different. People wear their hatreds like badges. And I don't know if that's any worse than wearing a disguise over them.

My friends and I, we grew up in the '60s, an idealistic lot. We consciously rejected the racism and bigotry that hovered so close to the surface in previous generations. Looking back, it wasn't because we thought our parents were bad people – they were good people. We just could see no place in the future for those old hatreds that came of generation after generation living in segregation.

But here we are now, living in a practically all-white, homogenized enclave where old evils are creeping in, wearing new masks.

We're raising our kids, trying to teach them the right things.

And yet, I wonder if we aren't up against a more dangerous set of racisms and bigotries than existed 30 years ago. Because 30 years ago everything was out in the open for us to see, right there in our own homes, and all we had to do was go outside our homes to see that other people were just other people.

But nowadays, it seems as if prejudices lurk in the shadows. And some of those shadows, perhaps, are within our own hearts.

We say we want our children to experience other cultures, to know other kinds of people so that fear of the unknown won't be a part of their world view.

And then a nagging voice slinks in and says, oh yeah? Is that what you want?

Or do you really want your kids to experience other cultures only so long as they're pretty much just like us?

Your teenager comes home listening to rap music. You hear the lyrics. They degrade women and perpetuate racism – lyrics that come out of an impoverished place where violence and bitterness grow like weeds in a fallow field.

Do you want your kid listening to this? Or do you wish they were listening to old Supremes records?

Your kids make friends with the children of the Latino civil engineer down the street and you think, that's cool. But how do we feel about their going to play at the homes of the migrant farm workers up the road?

We were after a world where race, creed or color were not factors. What we wound up trying to shape was a world where everyone was like us. So is it any surprise that intolerance has reached new heights?

You can see the signs everywhere. It's not just between races and religions. Among the middle classes – all the classes, for that matter – there is rampant intolerance for anything different from ourselves.

Intolerance for opposing viewpoints, for instance. People don't just disagree about politics now, they sneer at people of opposing viewpoints as if those people are foolish, corrupt or worse. Rational debate is obliterated by slogans and platitudes.

Up in Camino, near the road where my friend jogs over swastikas, a logging mill says it is closing. The mill workers don't see it as a business decision; they just blame the spotted owl and the "ecofreaks." They think the "ecofreaks" are stupid and dangerous. The Sheriff's Department hate-crimes unit has been put on full alert because of the death threats the environmentalists have received. And the environmentalists – they seem shocked and surprised to be targeted so. They don't see how anybody can fail to understand their view on forest policy. They think the "rednecks" are stupid and dangerous.

And the children absorb all this. And swastikas get scrawled on the pavement.

My crowd, we grew up thinking we knew how to make things better. It's time to rethink. We haven't made things better. We haven't even succeeded in defining what "better" would be.

This Year, Light a Candle for Peace

I went out to buy a gift today, but I did not find what I was looking for. In fact, I didn't even know what I was looking for.

All I found was a candle.

It has been that way lately. Material things have been no inspiration. Stuff just seems like stuff.

I know, I know. We're supposed to buy things. It's our patriotic duty, and if we don't buy things then the terrorists win, etc. and so forth. But somehow, it just doesn't seem meaningful to go out and trade my labor for fluffy sweaters and George Foreman fat fryers and binoculars and CD burners and slippers.

It seems as if Christmas has come too quickly this year. It's been coming too quickly every year. Holidays are beginning to flutter past me like tinsel in a gale.

Somehow, though, this year feels like an important one. It feels like a good time to slow things down, step out of the wind and take refuge in the company of people who mean the most to us.

After all, we saw what can happen: Anything can happen – anything at all. You could be stricken by a rare disease. You could be carried away by aliens. A plane could crash into your building.

I've always wanted to take a few days off at Christmas and just go visiting as many people as I could. There are way too many old friends I haven't seen. I don't know why we lose touch. There aren't any good excuses.

We have careers, but for most of us, we would bring more to our careers if we had good, strong friendships to help rekindle our spirits. We have kids to raise, but our kids' lives would be a lot richer if we exposed them more to our friends.

We have shopping to do – it's our patriotic duty – but who wouldn't trade a mall for an hour of conversation?

So today I rushed out to buy a gift at Arden Fair. I had been putting off the effort for weeks, dreading the crowded scene, the twinge I always get at the commercialization of a holy day. I was strolling in a bit of a daze, and all the store windows were blurring together, when I heard a voice call my name.

I turned around and there was a dear old friend. We hugged and then looked at each other sheepishly. Has it really been a year since we talked?

We caught up quickly and then had to go our separate ways, laughing again – sheepishly – at how long it would take before the guilt sets in for having once again broken our promises to keep in touch.

As she walked away, this annual exercise – wasting time in shopping malls when I ought to be going from one friend's door to another – seemed even more pointless than usual. I walked and wondered what to do next.

The only good gift I could think of were airline tickets so my family can get some adventure time together.

The kids will be gone soon. Only two more Decembers remain before the older one goes to college. The younger will leave two years after that.

It grieves me to think of them leaving so soon. I can't adapt. I still require them to leave carrots out on the lawn for Santa's reindeer on Christmas Eve; I still go out in the middle of the night and chew on those carrots so it'll look like reindeer came. My daughters can hardly believe I do this. But they know I can't adapt.

I didn't have the money today for a spontaneous gift like airline tickets. So I just kept walking the mall.

I used to be spontaneous. I was telling my kids the other day about a time before they were born – a time when my wife and I found ourselves with eight unexpected house guests on a December night. Two friends had shown up with a Canadian guy and a Swedish guy they had recently met. And I brought home a kid I'd met that day from Japan, who spoke no English but was riding his bike alone from the West Coast to the East Coast. Then came a knock on the door and we found three college students who were riding their bikes from the East Coast to the West Coast and had been given my name as a place where they might stay the night.

Hearing me tell this story, my kids just stared as if a reindeer was crawling out of my mouth. They couldn't picture me being that easygoing.

So I walked down the mall, and soon I found myself in a little shop that sells candles. And that's when lines from a bit of old prose came floating into my head. I have no idea who wrote it, but I still remembered the lines:

"Every year at about this time, the world lights a candle to peace. It is a universal gesture, immune to politics. It pays tribute to no narrow philosophy, materialistic or messianic. The candle, when ignited, does not detonate. It illuminates. It doesn't challenge the heavens in a thundering roar. It makes its plea in a steady flame, reflected in the eye of a wondering child, or the squint of an elder who has seen it all.

"The candle graces the menorah as it fits the tree. It is at home in all the windows of the world."

And it dawned on me what I needed to buy.

A simple candle. One that I can light for peace.

Love 'Em, Hate 'Em; the Olympics are Upon Us

The Olympics are, by now, in full control of several households in the United States, including mine.

This was a surprising development, since right up until the moment they began, I didn't think I was the least bit interested in the Olympics.

But, as usual, the excitement of the games, the plots and subplots, the mix of grand and grotesque, the gravity of the flame, has pulled us in like ... well, like anything that you can love and hate simultaneously.

We love watching the games because of the athletic prowess on display. Any skill that requires great dedication and concentration is a thing to be admired. And so instead of reading a good book or, perhaps, sleeping, we sit transfixed into the wee hours by things we would not otherwise contemplate. We are absorbed by weight lifting, volleyball, water polo – well, maybe not water polo.

And we are more than transfixed by those sports we have dabbled in ourselves – watching the flawless form and concentration it takes to win a swimming race by one-hundredth of a second, for instance, or to win a footrace against the fastest runners on earth.

But counterbalancing our love of the athletic prowess here is disdain approaching a hatred for the mentality of competition.

I'm not saying competition isn't healthy in proper dosages. But we too often display an unhealthy fascination with winners and losers. It reflects itself in the way the Olympics are covered – in this notion that only the medalists are worthy of reverence, as if getting to the Olympics in the first place wasn't victory enough.

The Olympics are supposed to be a celebration of human potential, but after the platitudes of the opening ceremonies are done and the networks take over, too much of that gets lost in who wins and who loses.

We love the human drama. Can you think of a more courageous achievement than what we saw in the triumphant pain of 18-year-old Kerri Strug? In that instant as she stood on one leg after "sticking" her vault for her team's gold medal in gymnastics, she knew it had to be at the expense of her personal goals. What an instant; even as her back arched and her arms reached up to the ovation, her wounded leg recoiled in pain – a cross between a rising phoenix and a delicate flamingo.

And yet we hate the smarmy accounts of these human dramas, and the tendency of broadcasters and writers to compare gymnasts to phoenixes and flamingos.

We love the beauty of those moments of pure sportsmanship, when Tutsis and Hutus embrace after the race.

But we hate the nationalism. The media spin can make the Olympics seem like war games. Or Nuremberg rallies. Us against the world. The hourly medal counts. The unctuous coverage of U.S. performers while athletes from elsewhere are ignored or patronized.

Look at the tone taken toward Michelle Smith. She wins three golds – the first Irishwoman ever to even win a medal in swimming. What a story. The networks ought to be sending cameras to her hometown. Instead, we get innuendo: So, Ms. Smith, how long have you been using steroids?

What we do get, however, by way of coverage of foreign athletes, is a camera crew sent to the distant hometown of a Chinese gymnast to tell us how the evil Communist empire has yanked a little girl away from her family for seven years. Former local TV personality Beth Ruyak, who did a lovely job reading the piece, left out important cultural context by neglecting to explain that the Chinese have been separating certain children from their families for thousands of years, whether it be to train for the opera or train as emperors. Of course, we do get coverage of foreign athletes if they are quaint – a dwarf weight lifter from Turkey, that's the ticket.

We love the pageantry. Pomp and circumstance, from the moment the torch was lit by Muhammad Ali – the century's most graceful athlete who ruled, and was consumed by, the century's most brutal sport.

We hate the commercialism. Egad, corporate logos on anything that moves. Even the injustice of having the centennial Olympics in Atlanta instead of in Athens where they belonged was a testament to the power of marketing. Atlanta bought the games. It did so with a huge capacity for sales revenues. And just as importantly, a huge capacity for blarney. (Nice bit, massaging Atlanta's temperature numbers so that, by including round-the-clock readings, the average daily temperature for the city in July comes out in the high 70s.)

Finally, while we hate getting sucked into the boob tube for three weeks, we love it, too.

I love gathering the neighborhood kids in the living room to watch an event that some of them have participated in – swim racing for my own kids, for example, gymnastics or soccer for others. I tell them stories of the nine games I've seen since I was 6 and the Olympics came into our living room from Rome in black and white. And then we watch as new stories emerge from the timeless leveling principle of athletics.

After the events, the kids decide, momentarily, that they too should grow up to be Olympic champions. They storm out to the pool, or they imitate the gymnasts with movements that seem a cross between Isadora Duncan and Quasimodo.

Most of all, we love and hate the Olympic spectacle because it is, basically, us. The Olympics and the way we perceive them are a snapshot of all that's good and bad about what we are in 1996.

We are commercialized and nationalized and trivialized. But we also are hopeful and graceful and determined. We are the corporate logos. But we also are the unextinguished flame.

Christmas Comes Early in Oak Park

Johnnie Sington sat by her dining room table at the end of the day and looked around at the house she's lived in for 21 years.

Life had suddenly changed. This carpet under her feet seemed unfamiliar. These walls weren't the same walls as when she woke up this morning. Her face bore the stunned look of someone who stopped believing in Santa Claus long ago and suddenly finds out there are reindeer on the roof.

But those weren't reindeer tromping around up there on the roof this day.

It was Bob Tate and Tim Lien and a couple dozen other people, celebrating Christmas in April.

All in all, about 60 people showed up at Johnnie's place off Stockton Boulevard a week ago last Saturday. Chief executive officers, construction foremen, lawyers, housewives, accountants, laborers, a neuroradiologist. All brought together by word of mouth.

They started arriving at 6 a.m., bleary eyed, bearing hammers and saws, shovels, paint brushes, tool boxes and hardware.

By the time the sun began to go down, they had rewired the entire house, repaired the electrical appliances, fixed the plumbing, installed new carpeting, painted the house inside and out, painted the garage, torn down a crumbling old shed. And they yanked every weed out of a yard that Johnnie had gradually stopped being able to care for since hurting her back in 1966 and losing her husband in 1980.

And there was the roof. They tore off four layers of old, leaky roofing, replaced rotting rafters and put a spanking new roof on the house in 12 hours.

"I don't believe it," Johnnie mumbled, bug-eyed from the day's hubbub. "I don't believe it."

"I don't think Johnnie's life has been based upon people doing wonderful things for her," said Tate, who heads the accounting firm Tate, Propp, Beggs & Sugimoto. "I don't think she knows what to think."

There were a few construction experts on hand to coordinate the effort, but most of the volunteers were amateurs. None was more amateurish than me. I was assigned to the roofing crew despite a deeply ingrained fear of heights that had me squatting around the rooftop like a constipated cat, trying my darnedest to stop dropping tools and/or my body onto the painters working below.

It was a wonderful day even if it did leave me slightly hunch-backed.

Tate spearheaded the whole thing over a bottle of wine one night with a few friends. They had worked before with groups like Habitat for Humanity, which builds low-income housing with volunteer labor, but they were looking for something different.

Tate had heard about a group called Christmas in April * USA, which each year gathers volunteers and material donations to renovate homes for people who are unable to do the work themselves. Since 1983, 37 Christmas in April programs across the country have repaired 4,800 homes for people who were referred through churches, synagogues, community of organizations and service groups. This year, a record-breaking 40,000 volunteers worked on 1,800 homes.

"I've been looking two years for something like this," Tate said. "'Something people in business could get involved in, see immediate results and know who they were helping."

Tate and his friends incorporated a non-profit, Christmas in April * Sacramento. They started calling other friends in the trades. People like Lien of Walker Donant & Co., a Davis homebuilder. Lien and his wife, Kim, jumped in as "house captains," rounding up volunteers and supplies.

"In some ways, it wasn't as much work as I thought it would be; in some ways, it was more," said Lien. "People were really eager to get involved."

A committee gathered referrals from Sacramento Housing and Redevelopment Agency, then went to people's houses, looking for someone truly in need. "Finding the right house was the hard part," Tate said.

They found Johnnie, a widow in Oak Park. Her house is fundamentally a good one, but it badly needed repairs she could neither make nor afford. She was having doubts about how long she'd be able to stay there, and she did not want to move.

"They called me on the phone and said they were trying to help some people that needed some help," Johnnie said. "They seemed like honest people."

So did Johnnie, so the committee selected her. But as the day was approaching, she learned how many people were coming and began having second thoughts. "I started to back down, but my daughter talked me out of it."

Then all those people showed up at dawn. For a day her house looked like a tornado hit it. Then they were all gone, off to a barbecue at Land Park.

"The neat thing about Christmas in April is that it all gets done in one day," Tate said. "Then it's done. You don't have to keep fund raising. You don't have to hire an administrative staff. It's done."

Next year, Tate's goal is to have 300 to 500 volunteers and to work on 10 houses.

As we all limped off, Johnnie's look was glazed but her heart was full. "It makes me feel good to have all this help," she said. "It gives me hope that I can go on living here."

Sharky Times We're Living In, Eh?

All these shark attacks on the Southeast coast of the United States are beginning to feel like an Alfred Hitchcock movie. Week after week, reports come in of people being used as appetizers in the surf.

Experts are quoted saying this really isn't an unusually bad year for shark attacks. There are just lots more people nowadays – and hence, lots more people in the ocean available as bait – than there used to be.

But still, you can't help but think something weird is going on, like in "The Birds."

Sharks are scary at a primal level because we humans are used to being the biggest predators. We don't like it when another creature takes that status away from us.

True, more people die of bee stings. And yes, driving Highway 50 at 75 mph has got to be more dangerous.

And ponder this: If you're a kid boogie-boarding on the beaches of the Southeast, you might be focusing all your attention on the shadows passing under the water, but a bigger danger is up there, over your head.

Last week, while the news was filled with shark attacks, three people surfing at Virginia Beach, Va., were struck by lightning.

One of them was "duck diving" his board to paddle under a

breaking wave. He provided too tempting a target, and a bolt of lightning hit his upturned butt.

Approximately 100 people die each year as a result of being struck by lightning in the United States alone, while fewer than five a year are killed by shark attacks.

And, although once in a blue moon you might hear of two people being attacked at the same time by sharks, as they were last week in North Carolina, consider what happened at Japan's Shonan Beach, near Tokyo, 15 years ago: One bolt of lightning hit 12 surfers, killing half of them.

But sharks – they get the headlines.

I have spent a lot of time contemplating sharks from a vulnerable position, floating in the ocean on a surfboard. Three times in my life I have literally fled the ocean after shark encounters. And many, many, many more times than that I have absolutely scared the bejabbers out of myself by imagining what was with me as I surfed in Northern California's "Red Triangle," the infamous breeding ground for the Great White.

And I can tell you this: There's a reason why they give us the creeps.

Sharks have eyeballs and they have teeth. They can hunt you and they can eat you.

Lightning, by comparison, seems serendipitous. If lightning hits you, it's dumb luck without a shred of malice aforethought. But sharks ...

On a gray foggy day, chasing waves through the waters of Año Nuevo, dangling your tootsies in the food chain like so many sausages, there are times when the only adjective that comes to mind is "sharky."

And whenever I find myself in sharky waters, I am reminded of a report I read once, from some researchers somewhere, that said sharks and human beings were the only two species known to share a certain type of enzyme, suggesting some sort of long-lost evolutionary link.

And that's another reason why sharks are scary. They're cousins.

But the real reason all these shark attacks are being brought to our attention, of course, is that it's been a slow summer for domestic news.

Let's see: We've got Gary Condit, another sleazy politician using his position to sexually exploit young women. Sort of a shark attack story in its own right.

We've got, oh yeah, a feeble economy and the corresponding, disappearing budget surplus. Aw, don't worry; Dubya's on top of it. Never mind that most of his tax rebates were used for credit card payments, or that experts say the guy has an IQ about equal to a hammerhead.

No, the news has been slow. But we've got sharks.

And with all this media attention, we'll soon have elected officials calling out for political action.

Nobody wants to be called soft on sharks.

Moderate Democrats will want to put nets around the public beaches.

Moderate Republicans will argue in favor of no public expenditures on nets. Let those who can afford to do so put their own nets up around their own private beaches.

Environmentalists will recommend we get all the humans out of the water.

The gun lobby will recommend we open fire. Not on the environmentalists – on the sharks. For now.

Conservatives will argue that we need to just let market forces work themselves out in the oceans, even if it costs us a few arms and legs.

Liberals will recommend we appease the sharks by imposing a tax of several arms and legs per household.

Happily, before we see congressional action, this too shall pass. The water will get cold, the kids will get back to school, and hurricanes and wildfires and layoffs and celebrities and other priorities will retake the headlines.

And the sharks can go back to their place in the lineup. Forgotten, for the moment, but ever lurking.

Like distant cousins.

Hurricane Iniki Was a Real Jerk

We all have our own pet peeves. One of mine is when newspaper headline writers give human attributes to natural disasters.

"Killer Earthquake Rocks Bay Area."

What, did the earthquake premeditate the thing? I can see it now: The earthquake skulking around in its subterranean hideout, a chip on its shoulder bigger than the San Andreas, trying to nudge loose some rocks and saying, "Geez, if I could just get this faultline to slip a bit, I could do in the doggone Bay Bridge."

It drives me nuts: "Murderous Tornado Strikes Iowa." "Furious Forest Fire Fries Fonkville." "Typhoon Assaults Guam with Malice Aforethought."

Every pet peeve, however, should come with an exception clause. So I'm invoking mine. In the case of Hurricane Iniki, which coldheartedly ransacked Kauai two weeks back, headline writers ought to be free to assign human attributes.

"Bitch Hurricane Does a Number on Wessman's Favorite Place."

(Or, for our feminist readers, "Lazy No-good Insensitive Bad-breath Hurricane Bastard Rapes Garden Isle.")

I've been going to Hawaii for years – eight or nine times, I think.

Oh, I've traveled other places too, but for some reason, I keep going back to the islands. When the world really piles up on me, I know I can always go hide away at Mrs. Kobayashi's little guest cottage on the north shore of Kauai. I can remember who I am there.

The first time I went was 1972. Just out of high school, in no mood for college. With a couple of surfing buddies, I bought a round-trip ticket, a machete and a raincoat. We headed for then-little-known Kauai, figuring we'd use the machetes to build a treehouse and spend the winter near Hanalei Bay. It didn't work out that way. We wound up camping out of a '55 Chevy for 10 weeks, moving around to wherever the waves were. Nobody objected. Kauai was undeveloped – the whole island had only one stop sign and smelled of white ginger. Wonderful.

Later, when I met my wife, we wound up going over whenever we could.

The hotel/condo scene was never for us. Kelli and I used to rent little Datsun trucks with campers on the back, from an outfit that was called Beach Boy Campers. It was great. Your hotel was wherever you stopped – usually in a beach park, sometimes up in the mountains.

It was always fun. Even the time I drove under a lowhanging branch and peeled the top of the camper back like a sardine can. (That became a serious problem three days later when the engine died and we spent the night in the middle of a rice field where they grew mosquitoes for export to Burma, but that's another story that my wife doesn't like to have told because her face wound up looking temporarily like a topographical map of the Himalayas.)

Anyway, we used to rent campers, and then after our first child arrived we decided that two or three weeks in a camper with baby diapers was bad planning. So we took to staying in private cottages that get rented out by the week, and on Kauai it was always Mrs. Kobayashi's guest house. Right on the beach. Perfect setting.

It was in our early camper days that the last big hurricane to hit Kauai blew in – Hurricane Iwa.

As I recall, it was October 1982 and our three-week visit was almost over. We were to fly out the next morning. There we were in our camper, and it didn't have a radio, so we didn't know why the skies seemed to be getting darker and more windy than usual.

Come morning, rain and wind were really hammering us. At the airport, we found out that Hurricane Iwa was expected to hit by mid-day. We boarded what was to be the most turbulent flight I've ever taken on a jetliner. The plane was falling into air pockets so deep that passengers were screaming bloody murder and I was spilling Bloody Marys. Mind you, it's not like me to spill Bloody Marys.

By the time we got to Frisco, Hurricane Iwa had hit Kauai. With malice aforethought.

We went back the following autumn, and the damage stunned us. The south side of the island, in particular, had been clobbered. Palm trees had been snapped, condos were boarded up. A lot of people's finances had been ruined. But it was still pleasant there. The locals had shrugged it off, Aloha style.

On that post-Iwa visit, we were over on the Big Island in a rented camper – this one had a radio – when we heard the news that a tropical storm was approaching with aspirations of becoming a hurricane.

I'd had a year to mull the fact that a Beach Boy camper is no place to be in a hurricane. These things were fairly flimsy. People kept peeling the roofs off.

So we parked in the basement of a building on hotel row. All night we waited, but the tropical storm petered out and never arrived. Phew.

And that was my last experience with malicious wind phenomena in the islands – with the exception of an eventful flight to Molokai on a small prop plane last year, which my children likened to a carnival ride.

Two weeks ago, I'm told, Hurricane Iniki made Hurricane Iwa look like mere flatulence. The whole island of Kauai was smashed. Ninety percent of the houses were damaged. Hotels were crunched. Power and phones down indefinitely. The macadamia groves were ruined.

I figure I owe it to the people there, who have been so kind on my visits, to send some cash to help out. Personally, I'd rather pinpoint my contribution than send it out in a blunderbuss approach. There's a Salvation Army office in the town of Koloa, smack in the middle of it all, that served 64,000 meals in the first 36 hours after the hurricane. That's where I'll send some dough. The address: P.O. Box 1869, Koloa HI 96756.

All of a sudden I know how those headline writers feel.
Hurricane Iniki was mean and rotten to the core. She must have been abused as a child.

City's Leaders Play Footsyball Instead of Hardball

A City Council meeting is turned into a huge pep rally. Cheerleaders shiver and jocks howl like wolves. Gregg Lukenbill moves messianically through a crowd whose level of adoration is normally reserved for promises of eternal life – not football.

Frankly, the entire spectacle last week, and over recent months as Sacramento's political leaders decided whether to throw themselves into the chase to lure the Raiders, was rather embarrassing. And the people who should be embarrassed are the politicians. They've ensconced themselves as dupes.

Generally speaking, government should not be in the habit of subsidizing private enterprise. In recent years here, however, subsidies have come into vogue. Perhaps it started with the Hyatt Regency hotel, or perhaps it started earlier with the donation of new zoning in North Natomas for the bribe of pro sports. But, at some point it became an accepted thing for private businesspeople to ask the city to help them make their fortunes. And now city politicos leap like jesters at the chance.

This is not some little city in West Virginia that needs to go begging for economic development. Sacramento has in recent years grown beyond its previous status as a branch town, a creditor city whose earnings were borrowed and used to build Los Angeles, San Francisco and Orange County. Ours might now be characterized as a debtor city, a place where money is being loaned to businesses that are tripping over themselves to be here.

Sacramento is in the catbird seat when it comes to economic

development. And for us, subsidies are no longer required to lure most business ventures.

That's not to say the city should never subsidize a private enterprise. But each time it's done, we must realize that we've made a precedent-setting policy decision, whatever the prospective return, and we must be sure that a deal simply will not otherwise work.

A good place for the city not to subsidize development, for instance, is on Lot A, the last prime piece of real estate on Capitol Mall. Three of the four finalists who would develop Lot A are asking for a subsidy. One, Lukenbill and Reliance Development Group, asks the city for $1 million a year toward a luxury hotel. Prudential Real Estate development and Teichert Land Co. ask for subsidies in two ways – $14.5 million for the hotel, and another $4 million taken off the ($13 million) assessed value of the land. Lankford & Cook would take a $4.5 million subsidy by paying only $8.5 million for the land. Only Rockefeller and Associates Realty, with Peter McCuen, asks for no subsidy.

Rockefeller can do this because it's a bigger outfit with a more long-term approach to investment. Its $241 million proposal wouldn't hit break-even for nearly a dozen years, as opposed to six or seven for the others. But when they're ready to sell, they'll have something much more grand – and so will the city. That Rockefeller would even be interested signals the desirability of Sacramento nationally. And desirability should bring with it choosiness about whom we play footsy with. Make that, footsyball.

Sacramento also is a desirable place for a National Football League franchise. But our politicians don't seem convinced. They negotiate like dweebs.

When you're the kid who owns the football, the other kids will let you play. If you're a dweeb, you'll accept their first offer and be a blocker. But if you're cool, you'll insist on being quarterback. (Egads, I've used a football analogy! I'm infected!)

Now, I am willing to admit that it is a good idea for this city to invest in attracting a football franchise. It's a cliche – and a sad statement on American culture – that an NFL franchise would help to signal Sacramento's ascendancy and trigger new investment by quality outfits like Rockefeller. (The down side is that such a process is inflationary for most of us who live here.) More importantly, an NFL team would give us something to do.

Bringing a football team may even be worth giving away $50 million, which is how much the Bee's headlines tell us we're asked to subsidize – and maybe even $122.3 million, which is how much we're really subsidizing by the time we'd retire debt on $50 million in bonds. I'm not convinced, but maybe.

It does rather nag at one, however, to subsidize the likes of Lukenbill and Joe Benvenuti in an enterprise that, you can bet, is going to make them a lot of new money. They claim to be risking millions of their own, but really, how much risk is there to guaranteeing ticket and concession sales? If the Kings can sell out nearly four years running, anything that grunts loud can sell out.

Moreover, this city already wrote a massive subsidy in North Natomas for the Sacramento Sports Association and a passel of other developers. The 1,461 developable acres in North Natomas, controlled by Benvenuti, Lukenbill and Sacramento Savings & Loan, were worth an estimated $43 million before they were rezoned and infrastructure put in. By last January, that land's estimated value had grown to $118 million, and was projected at $225 million in current dollars if all the planned infrastructure is built. Of course, half a ballpark must be built before full development will be allowed under terms of the city's zoning agreement, so for the Sports Association, a great deal more rides on getting a franchise than just the opportunity to sit in luxury boxes and root above the minions.

And then there's the unresolved issue of who's going to pay the $50 million required for drainage in the area.

And do you recall the last business transaction where you were told something would cost you nothing, then told it would cost you, say, $30 million, and then, making no counter offer, you were told the price had just gone up to $122 million – and you went along with it?

But aside from all that, it's the way in which they've approached negotiating that makes the City Council members look like fools.

It is foolish for the city to go waving $122 million at just one football franchise, particularly one that's run by the faithless Al Davis, a master at playing one municipality off another. (He's taken $20 million from Los Angeles and Irwindale, and won $33 million from Oakland in an antitrust suit.)

There are other football teams looking for new homes. At least three have made inquiries here, I'm told, since we started waving money at Al Davis. It's easy to look at the roster of NFL teams and come up with a few that would be willing to talk turkey: Tampa Bay's team has been lagging in attendance; the New England Patriots still don't have a stadium; the Buffalo Bills have been losing money, and who wouldn't want to leave Buffalo?

Mayor Anne Rudin ought to put together a good negotiating team and head back east, if for no other reason than for the message it will send Al Davis. If nothing else, she ought to check into a hotel in upstate New York for a while.

Put yourself in faithless Al's shoes.

The market for an NFL franchise extends about 65 miles in any direction. That places a Sacramento team's westernmost fans somewhere around Walnut Creek. If Davis moves his team back to Oakland, and Sacramento winds up getting someone else's NFL franchise, we've lopped off Contra Costa County from him. Because, let's face it, if you're leaving a stadium on a cold dark night after a football game, would you rather be leaving one in Oakland or in Sacramento? A competing team in Sacramento would leave him drawing an audience from a much smaller, less affluent crowd than he had before in Oakland.

For the same reason, if we wind up getting a team – the Bills or the Bucs, say – before Davis returns to Oakland, there will be no triumphant-return-of-the-wayward-son act for Davis in Oakland, which his ego so covets.

So far, City Manager Walt Slipe and finance man Tom Friery have left the door open for our elected officials, in their infinite wisdom, to negotiate with someone other than Davis. The documents that have been drawn up don't refer to the Raiders; they refer to an NFL team, in general.

The Bay Area's days as the one, dominant force in Northern California commerce are over. For nine quarters in a row, commercial leasing activity in the Sacramento metropolitan area has topped that of San Francisco. That hasn't happened since the Gold Rush.

This city should hang tough and let Al Davis know that if David Rockefeller knows a good thing when he sees it, so should the Raiders. And if the next NFL franchise in Northern California isn't the Raiders, too damned bad, Al.

Of Dogs and Daughters in This Cruel World

Some people live vicariously through their children.

They provide for their kids all that they never had as kids themselves. They prod their progeny toward glories they never experienced – in sports, in academia, in show business. They struggle off to work every day to bust their butts, wistful but serene in the knowledge that their children are living the good life.

Not me.

I live vicariously through my dog.

Basil Milkbone is his name, and he's got it made.

When I trudge off to work in the morning, it's not my daughters' existence I take comfort in. It's Basil's.

He will sleep in, a skill he has acquired with great practice. He will rise at about 9 a.m. and mosey over to the back door. He'll sit there staring out the glass, pondering the vastness of time and space, until somebody notices him and lets him out.

Whoever lets him out will probably be a kind and beautiful, intelligent female human being with blond hair. She will fondly stroke his Springer Spaniel coat and whisper how handsome and good he is. He will go outside and pee on a blooming rose bush, and then he will take a short nap, drifting off while admiring the branch structure of a California madrone.

At about the same time of day that I am being told off on the telephone by some gun fanatic who wants to cancel his subscription over an editorial cartoon drawn by somebody in Philadelphia, a sparrow will nudge Basil Milkbone awake. He will amble over toward the kids' swing set and make his bowels move. Then he'll make his way toward the back door, pausing at his bowl to finish some of last night's leftovers. When the beautiful blond female human beings see him at the door, they shall invite him in, cooing and purring over him as if he were Mel Gibson. He will share their brunch and charm them with his big brown eyes. They will brush his long locks and perhaps even shampoo him in the tub.

At about the same time of day that some infuriated person is ranting at me for something we've written that was too close for comfort, my dog will glide nonchalantly onto the bed and lay his head upon my pillow. He will dream of chasing birds.

Waking up as the blond females prepare to leave on some errand, he will slip out the front door with the cunning of a burglar. Unnoticed, he will make his way down the street and around the block to the bicycle trail. He will run down the trail, then cut through the woods, the wind blowing in his face, looking for the adventurous life – at about the same time of the day that I am staring down a deadline, perspiring.

He will see a girl cocker and engage in flirtations. I will step in the residue of a German Shepherd on my way out to the parking lot.

Basil will be waiting for me by the driveway when I pull in after a rough commute on the crowded, angry highway. He will wag his tail and grin and cavort and act as if life could get no better than this. And I of course will assure him that it could not. Later, when I am splayed out on the couch, he will bury his forehead against my leg. I will scratch his nose and he will drift off to sleep, waking only to move from one blond female's bed to another, until morning comes and it is time to sleep in again.

These are the things I always wanted. And I live them vicariously through my dog because I know that my children will probably never have them.

Few people ever attain the life of respect and abundant choices that Basil enjoys, of course, and even fewer of them are women.

I would not want to be my daughters.

My daughters – they face too many challenges, too many obstacles, too rough a world. Although I envy them their beauty and intelligence and youth and talent, I would not want to be them.

They will go to school and try to understand why all the injustices cannot be fixed. They will fend off a society that suggests constantly that women are not meant to be in positions of authority.

They will get better grades than the boys until they're in about the 10th grade, studies say. And then as the pressures of puberty mount, a system designed to build the self-confidence of adolescent boys and grind down the confidence of girls will distract and subvert them and they will buy into it, their grades will tail off – that is, unless they have some great inner strength.

I don't know what to do to give them that inner strength. I suppose the best thing is to always believe in them and to convince them that they must believe in themselves. But, damn, there are forces in their lives every day they've got to fend off.

The other day their mother asked them, "If you were going to draw a picture of someone really important, who would you draw?"

A doctor, the 7-year-old said. "Would the doctor be a man or a lady?" mother asked. "A man doctor with a lady nurse."

Geez, they get subliminal signals in everything they do.

The 5-year-old said she'd draw Santa Claus, God and the Tooth Fairy. Mother put off asking whether the latter two were gender-specific.

I want my children to grow up in a meritocracy, where the only limits to what they can accomplish are what they are able to accomplish. But damn, barring unforeseen intervention by Santa Claus, God and the Tooth Fairy, they've got to grow up fighting the odds.

So as much as I admire them – as much as they are my pride and joy – I don't envy them and I sure don't want to live vicariously through them.

Being a dog would be a lot easier. Heck, even being a male newspaper editor would be a cakewalk compared to what they're up against.

Clyde, Steve and Senator Quayle·

Meandering on a Friday night, I found myself sitting on a barstool next to an old friend, Clyde. Somehow the subject of alienation came up. Talk turned from his recent woes as a little guy in the construction business to his experience in Vietnam.

I lifted a cup to him as a veteran, without thinking much about it, really, and he raised an eyebrow.

"Where were you when I was coming home?" Clyde asked.

As a matter of fact, at about the time Clyde was coming home from Vietnam, I was trying to figure out what the hell I was going to do if I was drafted. I knew one thing: I didn't want anything to do with that war.

I didn't mention that to Clyde. It probably would have spoiled a good two-hour tale of his tour of duty.

It has become unfashionable of late to admit that you opposed the Vietnam War, that you didn't want to go, that you felt it was fundamentally wrong. The change in fashion has grown out of a rightful, and long-overdue, respect being accorded those who did serve in Vietnam.

In going out of our way to say thanks to those who went, however, many of us have chosen to be quiet about the reasons why we didn't want to go. In so doing, we are silent about lessons that shaped our lives.

Now we have the flight of Dan Quayle to ponder.

It turns out that the Republican vice presidential nominee was a rich kid who probably used his father's influence to get into the National Guard, lowering the odds he'd be shipped off to Southeast Asia.

Now, there is a certain irony and hypocrisy to a guy who has been so willing to carry the political banner of militarism, but who chose to carry a safety net 20 years ago when the heat was on.

There also is irony and hypocrisy, however, when 500 reporters gather like a righteous wolf pack on Quayle's front yard to assail him with questions as he's trying to take his garbage out. You can't help but wonder: How many of those guys wanted to fight in the 1960s?

A majority of them, like me, would have loved nothing better than to have been born the son of a rich man, and would not have hesitated at all to pull some of daddy's strings if it meant not going to that war.

And for many, it wasn't so much a lack of courage that made us look for ways out, any more than it was an act of courage that made others go. For both sides, ours were acts of innocence waiting to be shattered.

I was eligible for the Vietnam-era draft for only one year before it was stopped. I had grown up worrying about it, just as my older brother and all his friends did. I saw our friends go. Most came back. Others didn't. The war was on the evening news every night in red hues, and it was debated at the family dinner table at least once a week from 1966 until I moved out.

My year of eligibility was a lottery year: They pulled birthdays out of a barrel, and if your birthday was one of the first 100 or so drawn in the lottery, you'd be drafted. No Shirley Jackson short story could have been more foreboding.

My number was 267. Lucky 267. My roommate Steve, the brightest and best, wasn't so lucky. His number was 7. And Steve's father wasn't rich. He was a blue-collar man, a veteran himself, and had been a hawk on Vietnam – until his son's number came up 7.

When it happened, Steve and I and a bunch of other guys were sharing a house, starting college and generally bidding puberty adieu. We couldn't believe Steve's number. It was typical of his luck.

In an event also typical of his luck, Steve managed to get a six-month draft deferment – the hard way.

When he got a letter from his draft board telling him to report for a physical, we had a wild party. Steve drank too much tequila. He went out back to sit beneath a grape arbor and look up at the stars, and passed out cold. Meanwhile, one of our guests got in his car to leave, found it blockaded in the driveway by other cars, and chose to drive through the back yard. He ran over Steve in the process, but the driver didn't know it, and Steve slept right through it. Steve woke up in the morning flat on his face in the yard, unable to get up because both of his arms were broken. Since nobody was home, he had to hitchhike to the hospital, which isn't easy to do with two broken arms.

That was good for six months only. All it did was give Steve a lot more time to think about going to Vietnam. And the war, which was already repugnant to 52 percent of Americans, became even more repugnant to him.

I'd come home late and find Steve in the living room, rocking in a chair his father had given him, his arms in slings, drunkenly reading Shakespeare aloud, oblivious to my presence.

The time came and he had to make a decision. He went to Canada.

He went believing he could never again come home legally. He could not have parties with his chums. He could not read Shakespeare in his family's house late at night. He could not see his father.

The FBI came to our door but we didn't know just where Steve was. For a while word filtered down from the north. He was having a hard time of it in British Columbia. He didn't like the weather and couldn't find a good job. He was lonely for his people. There were reports that he'd gotten deeply into drugs.

The last time I saw him was in 1975, when by chance I picked him up hitchhiking on the Coast Highway. He was in the country illegally. He didn't seem the same, much as a lot of the guys who'd returned from Vietnam didn't seem the same. He, too, looked shell-shocked.

I dropped him off at his destination and we made arrangements to meet the next day. He didn't show up. I never saw him again.

So I'll lift a cup to Clyde the veteran, but I'll lift a cup to Steve the dodger, too. They were both soldiers of a time we're still trying to figure out – a time when patriotism and duty clashed headlong in our conscience with issues of tolerance and morality. We should not turn our backs on history by trading one dogma for another.

Courage is Trying to Make Things Normal

It is difficult to explain the extent to which something like a major earthquake can cause your sense of well-being to simply unravel.

Last week's images of Los Angeles – distorted as they were by the fact that TV cameras go only where the damage is worst – still conveyed a sense of a world turned over, under, sideways and down.

We saw people doing anything they could to restore a sense of normalcy. They lined up at the fast-food joints. They hit the coffee houses they usually hit. Partly they were hungry, but mainly they needed to do something that felt like normal life.

The looks on their faces were just like the looks of people who have been through wildfires or hurricanes. It is, to a far lesser extent, the same look – the same stunned, methodical motion – that you see in pictures of Sarajevo or Mogadishu. It is the look that says I must keep going, I must find solace in the luxury of routine.

That's it – that's what's behind the look: Routines that had seemed mundane and even bothersome the day before now assume a sense of luxury.

Last week's events dragged me back to October 1989. Very few experiences have jarred me the way I was jarred that day at the ballpark.

I paid a ridiculous price to a scalper for a ticket to what I figured might be a once-in-a-lifetime World Series game – the A's against the Giants. The ultimate match-up. The Bay Bridge Series. What transpired, of course, was more than I had bargained for.

At 5:04 p.m., half an hour before game time, while the whole country watched, Candlestick began to rock at magnitude 7.2. And for the longest 20 seconds imaginable, I stared at the concrete pillar that held the stadium's upper deck over my head. It felt as if I was peering into eternity.

So this is it, I thought. The baseball fan's ultimate death.

The moment the shaking stops and you realize you are still OK, you shift into a somnambulistic stride. It is as if you are sleepwalking. And as you sleepwalk, there is this tremendous instinct that seeks and insists upon a return to normalcy.

I remember vividly that at Candlestick that day, only minutes after the shaking stopped, thousands of people in the upper deck began to sing "We will, we will rock you!" For the vast majority of people there, the first order of business was to get on with things – to play the game. They weren't being crass; they were venting a gut-deep anxiety.

That sensation goes hand-in-hand with a strong homing instinct. After realizing that what had just happened was real – that some guy named Ernie wasn't up there fixing the lights and they weren't going to just play the game – I wanted to get home as soon as possible. Partly, I didn't want to be in the Bay Area anymore, since aftershocks were possible. But largely, I wanted to be surrounded by the familiar … as in "family."

A section of the Bay Bridge had collapsed and early radio reports indicated that other freeways were closed as well, so I decided to try to drive home by going straight through the city. It took four hours to get from Candlestick to the Golden Gate Bridge.

I'll never forget the strangeness of that night. The streetcars abandoned in the road. The darkened windows. The contrast between the vast majority of buildings that weren't visibly damaged, and the occasional rubble of brick where one had collapsed in a heap.

And mostly I recall the look on the faces of stunned people as they stood in line to buy batteries at hardware stores, or as they crowded into any eating establishment that had candles.

I don't think they were there because they were hungry, I think they were drawn to the light.

The last view I had of San Francisco that night was right after we'd crossed the Golden Gate Bridge. I looked back at the city from the Marin headlands. Normally, you get a glorious view of the city from there, but on this night all I could see was San Francisco's silhouette. And the only lights anywhere were the fires burning in the Marina district.

I didn't have to wake up in the Bay Area the next day. I didn't have to live with the low murmur of chaos and fear. I didn't have to find contractors to do repairs, or find new ways of getting to work.

I just went home, where things were normal.

Except they weren't normal. Because inside me, things had changed.

For a couple of months, I was a wreck. My emotions ran near the surface. My dreams were unpleasant. Sudden noises jarred me. Sudden motions – the kids jumping up on my bed – caused me to panic. And my post-traumatic stress was only enhanced by what I saw on the news – the views of collapsed overpasses, the tales of human tragedy and human bravery.

Those tales of bravery are the most intriguing thing of all. All those people – they have that look in spades.

Courage, I think, is doing what must be done when all you want is for things to be normal.

There is something about having a thing as solid as the earth just stand up and shake that simply undermines all your assumptions. And I suppose that if you come through it OK, there are lessons to be learned in there – lessons about the luxury of routines. And lessons about how any routine that can't be viewed as a luxury should be jettisoned.

I've Got to Get My Y2K Act Together

But seriously, sometimes I think I'm heading for a big letdown with this whole millennial deal.

Y2K is almost here. On the Armageddon-planning end of things, other than buying an extra pack of AA batteries, I am woefully unprepared. And when it comes to planning for partying on New Year's Eve, I haven't lifted a finger.

I'm not the only one. The sales of generators, water barrels and other emergency provisions have pretty much fizzled. And hotels and restaurants, come the night before Christmas, could be practically giving away the New Year's packages they'd hoped to sell for scalper prices.

These millenniums come around only every thousand years or so. You'd think we'd be taking this one a little more seriously.

Or maybe that's just the point. Maybe we are taking this seriously. All the hoopla about civilization collapsing, or all the hype about how we're all supposed to get out there and party hearty – maybe we've absorbed as much of it as we can. Maybe it's making us take a second look at what's important to us. And maybe, just maybe, what's important to us has been right under our noses all along.

Click your heels, Dorothy, and repeat after me: "There's no place like home. There's no place like home."

Crisis? What crisis? As to planning for emergency power outages and the complete breakdown of modern society as we know it and so forth, I can understand why lots of people are deciding to shine it on.

After all, people who live in urban areas don't get excited about buying generators and live chickens and 50-gallon water barrels. In city life, the sense that things will be provided – somehow, by someone – is keen. And besides, a flock of chickens violates the rules of most condominium associations.

But I have no excuse. I live in the mountains. When the power goes out, sometimes it's out for a long time. That presents problems. The most important one, socially speaking, is that without electricity, my well pumps don't work. And that means I can't take showers.

I have noticed that utility companies are not expressing absolute certainty that service will continue uninterrupted at the stroke of midnight. So you'd think that I'd have at least gotten off the dime and bought a generator.

Truth is, I thought about it. I even looked into it. But to buy a decent generator would have set me back $700 or so. And to have my house properly rewired so that the electricity I generate cannot back up into the grid and electrocute an innocent utility worker somewhere would have cost another $700 or so.

So I'm figuring, what the heck. I'll save the $1,400 and skip showers for a week or two. I'm sure after a few days, urban co-workers will be more than happy to invite me over for a shower. Maybe they'll have some canned goods to share.

I could use the $1,400 to plan an exciting New Year's Eve. I could use it as a down payment for a night at the Ritz in San Francisco, where three-day packages are priced at up to $100,000 – and will probably go on sale soon, since there were no takers as of Monday.

But for some reason I have been completely lax about New Year's Eve.

I have a couple of party invitations, so there will be friends and champagne – normally, a combination that can't be beat. Normally I would be tickled pinker than bubbly to have a couple of party invites.

But a year ago, my friends and I were so ambitious. We stood in the kitchen at a New Year's Eve party – why do we always gather in the kitchen? – and threw out ideas:

"I say Fiji for New Year's."

"Nah, too many airports. I say the desert."

"Yeah! How about camping in Baja?"

"Perfect! Camping in Baja it is!"

Except that nobody I know is going camping in Baja.

For most of the folks I know, the big Y2K New Year's has taken a surprisingly introspective twist.

Many seem to be deliberately planning quiet evenings at home with their families. Some are using the moment to re-examine their spiritual values. Still others appear content to get together with the same friends they always get together with, in the same kitchens, and mark the new millennium with a quiet celebration of the beauty of doing the things that are familiar and comfortable.

And you know, we might be onto something here.

Maybe the real power surge on New Year's Day will occur when millions of people decide to stop whining and start appreciating life and living it a little more fully.

It's human nature to look for ways to dog-ear the passage of time. We feel compelled to mark our progress – even if we don't always know exactly what it is we're supposed to be progressing to.

So every Jan. 1, we sing "Auld Lang Syne," we make resolutions, and we wear silly hats to show that we're actually very cavalier about it all.

But every thousand years or so, perhaps, we owe it to ourselves to sit down in a quiet place and decide how we feel about one another, and whether we're really making the most of this fortunate thing that is human life.

The View from Angelo's Perch

There is a little map our paper has put together that will make your jaw drop. It shows every major housing development in the region that has either won approval or is currently seeking approval.

But if you want to see where the path of development is going a decade from now, you need to stand before a much larger map – the one on the office wall of Sacramento's most influential real estate developer.

Angelo Tsakopoulos has been called lots of things. From scorn to praise, he tends to shrug them off.

Just don't call him a speculator.

"It's an insult," he says. "We never speculate."

Land speculators, in the real estate vernacular, do not develop land. They don't do the endless work required to line up entitlements and votes, roads, water and sewers, schools and utilities on a piece of raw land.

"They buy land right next to where we buy land in the hope they'll get a free ride," Tsakopoulos says.

Indeed, when he buys land, he's not gambling. He's painting in the map. "It's almost an art," he says.

From his first-floor office near California State University, Sacramento, Tsakopoulos commands a bird's-eye view of the region.

More than any other developer, he has been able to predict – indeed, to direct – the path of growth. His company, AKT Developments, has been in the thick of every major population push of the last three decades, from Roseville to Laguna to Natomas. Where his eyes turn, other eyes will follow.

Right now, his eyes are fixated on a huge swath of land just below Folsom, on the south side of Highway 50.

Commuters on that stupefying, congested stretch of highway will not be happy to hear it, but the likelihood is extremely high that the city of Folsom will jump the highway at upcoming annexation hearings, if for no other reason than that Tsakopoulos has concentrated all his energy on getting it done.

In the long run, you can set up all the urban service boundaries, ag preserves and open-space policies you want. If land can be bought by a developer, eventually it will be developed. To Tsakopoulos, it is as sure as history.

He keeps big placards near his desk, showing the path of growth over the centuries in cities like Philadelphia, New York and Chicago. "You can see that cities always grow along the transportation corridors," he says.

Another set of placards shows Sacramento, first in the 1880s, then the 1930s, the 1970s and today. The corridors between once-isolated towns – Roseville, Folsom, Davis, Dixon, Elk Grove – have rapidly filled in.

Now Tsakopoulos turns to the wall. One-third of it is taken up by a huge map of the region – a mosaic of aerial photos. He knows this map like the back of the hand he uses to trace tract after tract that AKT has either bought, optioned or rejected.

"Where will development go?" he asks rhetorically, gazing on the largely undeveloped southern half of Sacramento County.

Here is a huge piece of land near the county landfill. "We own it but we can't develop it. Nobody wants to live next to a dump," he says, adding, "They were supposed to close it six years ago." Such is his business. Often he must bank land for years, even decades, before he makes a dime.

Here are wetlands – quicksand for a developer. Over there is the Mather Airport flight path. Out by Aerojet, "the water's polluted."

Down near the Cosumnes, land is being bought by the Nature Conservancy for a greenbelt, because the only way to preserve open space is to own it.

He crosses off site after site until he's left standing with his finger on the tract just south of Folsom and Highway 50, north of White Rock Road and east of Scott Road.

It's the only major stretch of raw land with freeway frontage. Intel and Broadstone are right across the freeway. This is where the path of development is going next.

Highway 50, he agrees, is a mess. They're putting in some diamond lanes and light rail. "That will help – and for a long time," he says. But he's a bit of a social Darwinist. The worse the highways get, he says, the sooner people will learn to car pool and ride public transit.

The remaining two-thirds of his office wall is taken up by maps of a half-dozen major housing projects now under way. He is proud of the work he does. Providing a steady supply of new homes helps keep prices in check and the area's economy growing.

"Do you have time? Do you have an hour?" he asks. "We'll jump in the car and drive out to Stone Lakes."

But then his daughter, Eleni, walks in. She's president now of AKT, a family-run operation whose influence greatly exceeds the size of its 15-person staff. "Sorry to interrupt," she says. "There's something you need to see."

He leaves, shadowed by a grandson who's starting his first summer job. Soon he comes back, apologizing, joined now by son Kyriakos, a principal with the company.

Now his secretary comes in. The Secret Service is on the phone from his house with some questions.

"We're having Hillary Clinton over for lunch on Thursday," he smiles.

He's a poor farm kid from Greece who grew up to be powerful and wealthy. A Democrat in a prevalently Republican line of work. A land developer who often speaks fondly of the environment. A student of philosophy with an uncanny mind for numbers.

Just don't call him a speculator.

Out of My Car and Into the Train

For some time now, I've wanted to ride light rail to work. It was one of those things I kept putting off until we moved The Business Journal to a new office, which is just a short walk to a light-rail station.

So last week I started taking the train. A few conclusions:

• First, contrary to what I'd imagined, riding light rail costs me more money than driving – about 25 percent more. Bear in mind I am an extreme commuter: I come in from Placerville every day.

• Second, it costs me even more in time. Light rail's tracks currently just aren't long enough and it takes too long between trains to be very efficient, especially for extreme commuters. It takes me about 50 percent more time to ride light rail than to stay in my car.

• Third conclusion: I love riding the train. The stress level is so much lower than driving, it will probably add years to my life. You get to watch people, maybe chat a bit. You can read, or you can just day-dream. You don't have to worry about colliding with CHP cars. You get exercise walking to and from the terminals. And it makes you feel you're doing something for the planet by reducing your exhaust emissions.

The trick, then, is to figure out whether riding light rail is worth the premium you pay in time and money.

Getting started requires a day or two of orientation. My first outing was particularly disorienting. That's because, for one thing, I hadn't exactly armed myself with information before I started out. For another, RT Metro has some annoyingly inadequate methods for arming you with information if you, like me, wing it.

Take freeway signs. Please. I came down Highway 50 loosely aware that the first station was called Butterfield, but not sure where it was. I figured I'd see a sign that read, "Butterfield Light Rail Station, Next Exit." Instead, there was a little picture of a trolley with an arrow underneath it, placed where I just caught it in my peripheral vision as I whipped past the Bradshaw Road offramp at 75 mph – er, uh, 55 mph.

Signage isn't any better once you're off the freeway. The first station I found was actually the third station on the line, Watt/Manlove. (Bear in mind I'm a slow learner. The first time I ever played golf, it took four swings before I hit the ball off the first tee.) (I've since cut that down to two swings.)

At the station I expected to find a pamphlet – "All About Riding Light Rail" – like you get at Bay Area Rapid Transit stations. But there aren't any pamphlets, only maps and mildly confusing signs telling you how to buy a ticket.

With a little advice, I soon figured out how to use the ticket machine, and with a little luck, I was carrying a $1 bill. The machine requires exact change, and the change machine handles nothing larger than a one.

I was surprised at the high fare – $1 during peak commuter hours for a ticket that's good for 90 minutes; 85 cents for the same ticket during less congested hours. I had expected a staggered rate structure, where your fare would be based on how far you rode.

After a couple of days I found there is something of a staggered fare for those who want to ride in the central part of the city during the middle of the day. Within the downtown-midtown district at midday, it only costs 25 cents for a 90-minute ticket. This is important for me, since my workaday routine includes a lunchtime jaunt to a health club, just one train station away. I didn't want to pay 85 cents just to get from 23rd Street to 29th Street, but I didn't want to walk.

So my daily cost of train fare is $2.25 – $1 to ride in, 25 cents at lunch and $1 to ride back out of town.

If I drive, my normal costs for a 100-mile round-trip commute are about $5 a day, figuring $1.25 a gallon and 25 miles to the gallon. (I don't pay for parking.)

When I take light rail, I'm traveling on 10 miles of track. That takes 20 miles a day off my commute, bringing my gas cost down to $4. When you add the train fare, I'm paying $6.25 a day on light rail.

In short, to commute 20 days a month, it costs me about $100 a month by car. On light rail, it costs $125.

OK. Wait a minute. You can buy a one-month RT pass for $40. That knocks my cost of using RT down to $120 a month – only 20 percent higher than by car. But I'd have to ride at least 17 days a month to make the pass pay for itself. At least two days a week, I have meetings outside the office that make a car necessary. Forget the pass.

Timewise, it generally takes me 50 minutes to drive to work, although traffic can make that go way up.

On light rail, it takes a couple of minutes to get off the freeway, park and walk to the rail terminal. I spend about 10 minutes waiting for the train to start rolling, with me in it, at Butterfield. The ride in takes about 15 minutes – typically, five minutes slower than driving. The walk to my office takes eight minutes. In all, about an hour and 15 minutes instead of 50 minutes, and I won't even figure in the time spent walking to and from terminals at lunch.

So last Monday, after a week of riding light rail, I'm driving in my car, approaching the Bradshaw exit. I'm doing all this math in my head, trying to figure out what the costs will be when they extend the line to Folsom, and if they had a staggered rate structure, and if gas prices go up or down, and if I have to start paying for parking. And then I start factoring in the cost of maintenance on my car. And then I start factoring the cost of shoes I'll wear out doing all that walking. And the emotional costs of spending 50 minutes less each day at home. And the extra years added to my life … And the next thing I know, I've passed the train station and find myself on P Street, almost to work …

And the next thing I know, some motorcycle cop with a radar gun has clocked me going 40 in a 30-mph zone, and I'm getting a ticket.

That settles it. I'm taking the train.

"A Two-Tailed Crawdad? Really?"

Of Sports, Skiing, Work and Life in the Sun

Golf: Things I Get and Things I Don't

As the mercury began to gurgle like boiling brain cells in triple-digit heat last weekend, I found myself inexplicably staggering around a golf course in midday sun.

For the second day in a row.

And I knew at that moment that despite my best intentions, I had become a golfer.

I find myself intrigued by the game's nuances. That is, once in a while I hit a good shot and I'm intrigued by how it might have happened.

There is still much that I don't get about golf. But my list of "don't gets" is offset by a growing list of "do gets."

For example, I do get the Immutable Law of Escalating Purchases. When your game is sucking wind, you must purchase more equipment. A new pair of golf shoes can shave strokes from your score, but only for a few rounds. When the new shoes wear off, a new glove might get you through one more round before a new putter is required. However, you cannot cheat the golf gods by offering up shoddy equipment. Your sacrifice must be costly. My recent purchase of a $13 driver from Price Club neither appeased nor amused the gods.

Then again, I still do not get those fuzzy covers people put on their woods. Golf clubs are designed to crash into golf balls at speeds exceeding 100 mph, without air bags. Why cover them? Are they going to hurt themselves cavorting in the trunk of your car? Might they contract a social disease if left to fraternize unchaperoned with the irons? Is that what those are? Golf club condoms?

I do get the reason why golf's library is full of joke books and guides to cheating. Why would anybody play this game who could not take a joke? Everything about the game is intended to hurt your feelings.

I played with an accountant until he grew huffy at my habit of kicking the ball out from behind oak trees. This is an important part of my game; take it away and traffic backs up on the course. I now play with people who enjoy the finer points of the game, such as the many subtle rulings on Mulligans, Provisional Mulligans, and Double Provisional IRA Terrorist Exploding Ball Mulligans.

I don't get the idea that people conduct business on golf courses. I don't even understand how people have conversations on golf courses.

Off the course, I talk to my golf chums about everything from business to metaphysics. But we never talk about those things on the golf course. We convene at the tee, where there is a minute or two of hushed strategizing before it's your turn to hit the ball. Each person swings, and then we're walking to find our balls. That often means going in separate directions. For me, it usually means walking off alone into the woods on the right.

We reconvene on the putting green. Perhaps the good golfers get in a few deals, waiting there for us bad golfers, but I doubt it. On the few times when I got there first, all I wanted to talk about was how this thing had happened.

Perhaps the notion that business is conducted on the course is simply an image carefully devised to make spouses, non-golfing associates and tax auditors believe something important is going on.

And here we come to the part of golf that I really don't get: the preoccupation of golf with its own image.

In a column a year ago, while grousing about middle age, I besmirched the game. I soon learned that golfers are sensitive about the sport's snobbish image. They get testy when it is called a game of the moneyed elite, and some of them will have their servants take a letter, scolding you.

Frankly, there are wide gaps between golf's image of itself and the image held by the rest of humanity.

My wife is a good barometer of the rest of humanity. She is astounded at my interest in golf. Overnight she thinks, I've gone old on her. She fully expects me to show up in lime-green polyester pants, white shoes and matching Naugahyde belt. (OK, if it pleases the gods.)

Confronted with my wife's perceptions, I find myself – like

those golfers who scolded me in letters – defensive about the image of the game.

"No, no," I tell her, "it's not like that. At least, not on the public courses where they are required to let me play."

Of course, it is not on the public courses but on the private ones where the game's image is most fiercely defended. And on some of those courses, my wife's teasing about golf would become outright hostility if she knew what really goes on.

Golf's private clubs are described as "the last caste system in America" in a new book by Marcia Chambers, "The Unplayable Lie: The Untold Story of Women and Discrimination in American Golf." While that's not an accurate statement – America has a big and growing list of caste systems – it's true that golf continues to tolerate an inbred male chauvinism.

Witness the recent controversies over Rocklin's gorgeous Granite Bay Country Club.

Membership at Granite Bay, I am told, runs in the neighborhood of $45,000. You pay the same whether you're male or female. And yet the club's developers made the incredible blunder of building one luxurious clubroom for men and a separate, less luxurious clubroom for women. How can you make that kind of a screwup in the '90s unless you have absolutely no idea of how the rest of humanity views the game?

There is an insidious nature to golf which can gradually make diehards insensitive – OK, dumb – to its flawed traditions. As your skill grows, your affection for the game grows, but so too grows the sentimental fog through which you view the game's image.

As I have become able to predict where several of my shots will end up (generally, in the trees on the right), I also have grown more tolerant of the game's quirks – and more gullible about the game's "mystique."

I even become willing to accept that there might be some reason to require that men's shirts have collars.

This summer, however, as I stagger down 100-degree fairways, I hope that my handicap does not hit a point where I am able to overlook discrimination.

I have two daughters. I'd like to think their money will be good for full privileges at any country club in the nation. And then, if they want to run around with fuzzy condoms on their woods, I say let 'em.

The Tyranny of Our First Sunny Day

It is Sunday morning. I am trying to catch up on my sleep, but it isn't working. Something weird is going on.

"That's the sun," my wife says. "It's shining in through the window."

The sun? The sun? You're telling me the sun, which hasn't had the common decency to show its face all spring, has decided to show up now? On the first morning I've had in weeks for sleeping in? On the morning after a party where the wine made us all act goofy? Like some errant cousin, the sun just shows up?

"It wants you to come out and play," she says, handing me a glass of orange juice.

I squish my winter-blubber body into a T-shirt and a pair of shorts that have apparently shrunk in the dryer, and I fumble out back to the patio.

Arghh! What are those? Those – those white things?

"Those are your feet," she explains.

My bare feet twinkle down there at the end of my blubbery legs, as white as the skin where you peel off a Band-Aid.

"My feet? What do they want?"

"They want you to take them jogging."

I was afraid she was going to say that.

As recently as last November, I was in fantastic shape. My family had just enjoyed a summer full of adventures and activities. We had spent several weeks by the ocean, swimming and snorkeling and playing in the waves up and down the West Coast, frolicking in the warm water of El Niño.

That was the good part of El Niño.

Then came the 100 rainy days. And a flood of work. More work than any of us knew what to do with – school work, and job work, and volunteer work, and hobby work, and work work work.

And somewhere along the line, my physical self became as languid as the tropical waters off the coast of South America when the equatorial wind refuses to blow.

Now, my white Band-Aid feet twinkle at the bottom of my winter-blubber legs, wanting me to take them out for a jog.

No excuses. The work is done. The spring wind has blown away my list of things to do. The calendar is clear. And so is the sky. The sun – if that's what woke me up – is out.

My wife brings me the old jogging shoes.

My stomach protests. Wait a minute, it says. Shouldn't we eat something first? Something like what we've been eating for this long winter's hibernation – you know, full of fat and stuff?

"You need to stop listening to your stomach," my wife says. "It is a liar."

Everything that my wife knows about the treachery of stomachs, she has learned from me. She has no firsthand experience. She is one of those people who never gains an ounce of weight, whether she exercises or not. She is as slender and pretty as the day she married me 14 years ago. The same cannot be said for me, however, and she has not an ounce of sympathy.

She shoves me out the gate.

There is a popular path that runs behind my house. I lurch toward it, my eyes squinting in the weird sunlight.

Haltingly, my feet begin to trot. My lungs begin to huff. My heart begins to beat and screech like a wiper on a bone-dry windshield. Volcanoes of sweat mix with the pollen that swarms in the air, making cakes on my face. My eyes begin to water.

Through the blurry pollen soup that coats my eyes, I can make out the others like me – dozens of blubbery Band-Aid white things, huffing and puffing and churning up the path.

Some are running. Some are walking. Some are on bicycles, their blubbery white faces bulging out of silly little helmets that have apparently shrunk in the dryer.

We grunt salutations as we pass one another:

"Mlurrrphh,"

"Shlurggish mlurrrphh."

It is a glorious day, green and bright, lit afire with wild blue lupines and screaming golden poppies and shrieking yellow scotchbroom. The kind of day we knew would come eventually.

Somehow, I wasn't ready for it. My sinuses are flowing now, like faucets. Every corpuscle in my body screams "hammock! ham-mock! ham-mock!"

Or maybe it's "ham-hock! ham-hock! ham-hock!"

I put my head down and keep running.

All of the other fatsos put their heads down and keep running, too.

Rivulets of sweat run down our bodies. The rivulets spill onto the pathway, forming brooks, babbling creeks, rushing streams, swirling tributaries and surging rivers. Whole torrents of sweat pour into the storm drains, boil through the levees and cascade over the dams.

The long-awaited floods of El Niño have finally arrived.

Can't Keep Our Hands Off Baseball

Proof that you don't have to be a baseball fan to have a swell time at a Sacramento River Cats game was sitting next to me on Opening Night at Raley Field.

My wife – who thinks pro sports are a metaphor for warfare in a male-dominated, chauvinist society – was grinning from ear to ear.

Pitcher Ariel Prieto was on the mound. The Edmonton Trappers had runners on first and third.

"There!" she exclaimed. "He grabbed his crotch again! That's nine times this at-bat!"

Yes, there's something for everybody at Raley Field.

Her discovery that pitcher Ariel Prieto compulsively adjusts his jock strap when he has runners on base was, for my wife, one of those sublime revelations that slowly unfold unto the patient observer during the meandering course of a baseball game – the esoteric kind of tidbit that makes philosophers and historians wax poetic during public television documentaries by Ken Burns.

Ah yes. We're a baseball town again. Poetry and metaphor will run amok in River City. That is, a laid-back, sort of goofy, Triple-A kind of poetry and metaphor.

Pro baseball has been a long time coming back to town. The big question is, how long will it stay this strong? The Cats sold 600,000 tickets before the first crotch was ever scratched.

Judging from the fun atmosphere that filled our nifty little ballyard by the river on Monday night, Triple-A baseball fever could be a long time here.

Of course, there are a few cures that need to be made right away if the Cats are going to keep their cool.

First, they've got to speed up the food thing. It took us a total of 45 minutes to score a dawg on opening night.

Second, they're going to have to get rid of the "YMCA" song during the seventh-inning stretch. I mean, the Village People? There could be violence.

And third, they're going to have to get their act together with the scoreboard. It was comical to watch how often the scorekeeper was playing catch-up.

Speaking of the scoreboard, maybe in order to keep a fan base broad enough to include the likes of my wife, they should add a crotch-scratching column. Like the philosophers say, baseball is a game of statistics.

Statisticians and historians shall note that Monday night's opener was very nearly besmirched by rain.

"You gotta be outta your mind," was my wife's response when I called home two hours before the game to assure her that we should go. "You are definitely outta your mind," she growled later as we approached the ballpark amid thunder, lightning and a deluge of rain.

We parked in Old Sac. The rain stopped. "It's meant to be," I said. "You're meant to be locked up," she said.

I strongly recommend strolling across Tower Bridge to the ballpark. Finding a parking spot was easier than finding a puddle. And the walk is wonderful. In the early evening, the bridge was a lovely ocher and the river was dark green. Ahead, the lights of Raley Field twinkled like the midway at a country fair. Our paces quickened as we approached the gate and got our first striking glimpse of the deep green diamond.

Smiling union organizers handed us fliers as we filed past, as if they were just another pregame festivity.

The stadium is not overwhelming. Architecturally, it has about the same number of embellishments as a strip mall in Roseville. But from the inside, its beauty shines through. The diamond is in plain view from every angle in the house. And the backdrop is absolutely wonderful. Over the right-center field wall is Tower Bridge. Toward right is the downtown skyline, with the Emerald Tower, the Wells building, Darth Vader and the county jail. Off to the left is the brightly lit Money Store pyramid – ziggurat – whatever. And down the right-field line, on the West Sac side of the river, is the topper – a ratty old metal industrial building that belongs to the California Dehydrating Co.

Perfect, somehow. The stadium is perfect.

We missed most of the pregame festivities by waiting in line for dawgs. After a 25-minute wait we hadn't moved at all, so we shrugged it off and went back to our seats.

We got there just in time to watch three skydivers bail out among the thunderclouds high above the stadium and spiral slowly down. Every one of us gaped breathlessly, waiting for lightning to flambé the skydivers.

But the Cats were blessed this night. No skydivers were zapped. No more rain fell. Nobody was hurt when eight dignitaries simultaneously threw out the ceremonial first pitch. Nobody jumped up and throttled the "on-field announcer," Rocko RioGato. Nobody yanked on the tail of Dinger, the team mascot. Nobody tripped Tim Busfield as he paraded out with a pair of beauty queens.

We didn't even care when we went back for a dawg in the fourth inning and couldn't return until the seventh.

Cynicism was in suspension on opening night.

And so it came to pass that the fans sitting around us allowed my wife to live when, after a couple beers and not enough dawgs, she began calling out the play-by-play on Ariel Prieto in a tone normally reserved for umpires.

"Some guys just can't keep their hands off it!" she hollered.

And she's right, of course. We can't keep our hands off baseball.

Surf's Up:
Mid-Life Crisis No. 42

It is dawn at a place called Salt Creek on a September day in 1971. The ocean is as smooth as cellophane. I am alone but for the pelicans.

I swing my surfboard toward shore, and with three strong strokes I am hurtling down the face of a 7-foot wave. Rising to my feet, every tendon leans into a bottom turn. The wave explodes behind me, and I am 17 years old, flying as if fired from a slingshot into the Elysian Fields ...

But that was a long time ago – back when "surfing" involved the firing of synapses, not microprocessors.

I was young, and I never thought a day would come when I would not surf. I didn't know the price of giving up things you love.

The surfing life, for me, was nothing like Hollywood's "totally, dude" stereotype. To surf well, you had to be there, ready and able, when the waves came. That meant living with a heightened sense of oceanic rhythms – the tides, the winds, the weather in faraway places.

Early to bed, early to rise. Listen for the size of the swell. Listen for the breeze in the trees. If the branches scrape the house, then the wind is onshore and the sea will be choppy and you'll do something else. But if the branches do not scrape the house, then perhaps an off-shore breeze will hold up the faces of waves until they peel off with perfect, ruler-straight edges. If that's what you hear, then hurry, for the conditions will not wait.

Of course, living at the ocean's beck and call leaves little room for other pursuits – things like education, jobs, families and other activities that require key chains.

I never consciously quit. My key chain filled up, somehow, and circumstances nudged me away from the sea.

At Salt Creek, while I had my back turned, they built a Ritz Carlton.

• • •

It is midafternoon on the island of Kauai in January 1988. I have paddled half a mile out to this spot the surfers call Middle of the Bay.

From the porch of our vacation rental in Hanalei, the waves looked as if they were 4 to 6 feet. But now that I am out here, it's clear that my sense of oceanic rhythms has grown rusty.

The waves are water mountains – 15-foot swells generated by storms in the distant Aleutians. They have grown angry in their long journey, and now they lurch over the reef like elephants, powerful enough to snap my pasty 34-year-old body into small bits of shark chum.

Paddling hard against the current just to stay in one place, I watch surfers ride these brutes for a few minutes. Suddenly, panic surges over me. What am I doing here? I begin paddling back in, and realize I am in a riptide, being poured toward the wide-open Pacific like a gnat at a picnic is poured from a pitcher of lemonade.

This surfboard used to float me fine, but now it's two inches under water as I paddle.

The beach and my vacation rental is half a mile away. The wife and kids are on the porch, unaware that Dad is out there in the bay, locked in a struggle to survive. Inching my way in, paddling as hard as I can, my muscles weaken. Sitting at a typewriter has done little to strengthen the latissimus dorsi.

It feels as if my arms are filled with sand. What they're really filled with is life's baggage.

Over the last 17 years, my pilgrimages to the ocean have been less and less frequent. Gradually, surfing has been relegated to vacations on the coast, or here in Hawaii, which has the strongest waves in the world.

The strongest waves in the world are a ridiculous place to be caught with bags of sand where your muscles are supposed to be. It is not a good place to be wearing contact lenses, either. Nor is it a good place to be if you have no idea whether the tide is coming or going.

My spirit recognizes this place, but my body has no clue. Ninety minutes later, I wash up on the beach.

• • •

Eight years later, in April 1996, it is twilight at a little point break near Poipu, on the gentle south shore of Kauai. The setting sun has sprinkled a molten ocean with shattered diamonds.

A soft offshore breeze causes 4-foot waves to peel off perfectly, and as each wave breaks, a prism is reflected in the blowing spray.

I have spent the last nine days surfing. Three times every day, I have paddled out, determined to stay out a little longer each time, gradually building my strength.

So far, I haven't caught many waves, and haven't looked like Nureyev on those I caught. Some waves have caught me. But gradually, the strength is returning.

It is backed by the strength of conviction that somewhere along the road, I made a mistake. I stopped doing something I loved.

I am here, for a precious moment, in a place where I once spent countless hundreds of hours. It has cost me 25 years of hard labor to get back.

A crisp 5-foot wave approaches the reef and begins to peak, right in front of me. The Poipu surfer kids are all 30 yards away. There is nobody here but me.

Nobody.

I turn toward shore. With six heaving, huffing strokes, I am hurtling down the face. My rusty old instincts click in, and I rise to my feet in time to carve the bottom turn. Every tendon is engaged.

The wave explodes behind me, and I am 42 years old, flying as if fired from a slingshot into the Elysian Fields.

Still Pained by Teen Peer Pressure

I'm flying! The Sierra's wintry white skies splay out above me like an Imax movie. And now my feet come into view, twisting, attached to a blue snowboard.

This is not going to end pretty.

Pain. That's all that comes of trying to keep up with teenagers.

It was painful back when I was a teen myself, trying to keep up with the others and be cool and not feel like a dork with my face erupting and my testosterone thumping and my intellect groping. And it's painful now.

This morning, well before what a teenager would call the butt-crack of dawn, I traveled into the mountains with my daughter's high-school ski and snowboard team. I vowed to keep up. Dumb adolescent move.

The ski/board team is a big deal at El Dorado High in Placerville. The school tends to get beat up on the football field and elbowed out at basketball. But when it comes to the slopes, El Dorado – alma mater of the late, lamented Spider Sabich – dominates.

Many of the 60 or 70 kids on the team are from families that originally moved to the Sierra for love of mountain sports. These kids grew up gliding on snow.

Me too. I came here to ski. And ski I did, for 25 years. Then, a few years back, I switched to snowboarding. I was bored with skiing, and besides, I wanted to keep up with my kids.

I learned fast – painfully fast. The first few days are brutal. But after the initial pulverizing, snowboarding is easier to master than skiing. Soon, I was carving huge turns, having a blast. And I was waiting, as I had always waited, for my kids to catch up.

That changed last year. I stopped waiting for my kids to catch up when Rachel joined the high school team. She quickly left me in her frozen white dust.

Small wonder. After tough workouts all week, they get up every Saturday and Sunday at 5 a.m., climb on a crowded bus and are riding the lifts at Heavenly by 8. They run gates and romp on the mountain. Then they race on Mondays for seven weeks. They get good, which tends to happen with anything that you have the time of your life doing.

So last season I went up with the team and was flabbergasted. My kid blew me off the mountain. I mean, she lapped me. She had to wait for me as if I were a child.

It was the first time I had ever been solidly thrashed in anything by one of my kids.

This year I was determined not to be left so far in the dust. For a couple of weeks I did knee-bends and sit-ups.

I sensed, however, that my daughter was only getting faster. One sign of this is that a love of speed seems to be creeping into other aspects of her life. For example, she's been learning to drive a car lately. She thinks the speed limit is meant to be ironic.

So anyway, this morning I came up to watch the team get ready for its first race of the season. And not so much to watch them, really, but to try to keep up with them.

From the first run, I knew I was kidding myself. As I carved my way down at what I thought was sizzling speed, meteors in blue and white team jackets blazed past me.

"This way, Dad," Rachel called as she led me toward the race course.

And then she was gone. Fog and blowing snow swirled into my goggles. Somewhere out there was a bullet flying down the mountain who was my kid.

Eventually, huffing and puffing, feet and thighs burning, I came upon her as she waited nonchalantly. The look on her face previewed the way she'll look someday when she decides whether to buy me a walker.

"It's just down around the bend, Dad. You OK?"

"Shlurrff hunnn – realllly grimphhgy fasshhhht."

"OK, well meet me at the top of Yahoo."

At the top of a run called Yahoo, the team had gathered. One by one, they charged the course. When her turn came, I watched my daughter fly lightly over the snow like a deer darts through the forest, using loopholes in the law of gravity.

My daughter's life fluttered past my eyes: eyes popping open for the first time and looking straight at me … carrying her on my back for evening walks by the river … first steps across a new carpet … potty training … training wheels … ballet recitals … arithmetic … braces … the first zit … a rumor of brassieres … a date to the Homecoming dance … laughter – always the laughter.

I have to stop before my eyelids freeze shut.

I can't let her leave me behind this way.

The course is clear now. All the kids have raced down. I glance over at a coach. "Go ahead," he says.

A knowing lump clusters in my throat. I should not do this – but before I can back down, I shove off.

The snow is fresh and easy to carve. The first gate rushes up fast, then the second, then the third …

Somewhere beneath the fresh snow, a jagged tooth of ice smirks up and bites the edge of my board. The mountain hurls me like an Australian dwarf.

Now the white sky and tree tops frame my boots and board as I twist through the air in Imax slow motion.

A familiar little girl's voice floats into my head. "Daddy, catch me!"

And then the pain.

Why I'm No Longer a Boxer

It's always neat to hear about people who are chasing their dreams, no matter what the odds. When they're young, the stories have the extra element of promise. You know much of what is going to happen is still ahead.

When I recently read about a young Sacramento woman who'd taken up boxing, it conjured up memories of a short period in my life when I, too became fascinated by the sport.

I'm not much fascinated by it anymore. Too many years of trying to purge the violence from my own soul, I guess, have left it difficult for me to watch a boxing match.

But there was a time when I was intrigued by pugilism. It started when I was in seventh grade and I got in a fist fight with a kid named Randy Cosette.

Randy was a cocky little red-headed guy, an inch or two shorter than me. Our disagreement began in wood shop – I think it had something to do with sawdust. By the end of class, we were puffing our chests out and circling each other like a couple of little baboons.

I "chose him off." We would meet for a duel after school across the street at the Tastee Freeze.

By the end of the day, word was out. "Wessman's going to fight Cosette" went through the school like some sort of subterranean drumbeat. They were taking odds, and because I was the taller of two runts, I was the favorite.

I remember walking to the Tastee Freeze in front of a throng of supporters, practically lifted off my feet by their enthusiasm. My entourage was worthy of Muhammad Ali. "You can take him!" they were shouting. "Kick his ass!"

There was Randy and his small group, waiting by the back wall of the Tastee Freeze, pacing, sneering.

I stepped up and immediately a ring of kids encircled us. There must have been a hundred of them. I took a swing with a roundhouse right, and – this was the eeriest thing – Randy just grinned.

That's when it dawned on me that I didn't know a thing about fighting. And Randy did. And he saw that I didn't.

He started ramming in jabs and right crosses, firing away at will, his punches like pistons landing with precision inside of my flailing, misdirected, lollipop lobs.

The next thing I knew, he had beaten the absolute bejabbers out of me. I was sprawled out on the cement, my nose spouting like a blowhole.

Through the ringing in my ears, I could detect a stunned silence at the Tastee Freeze. From my bleary vantage down on the pavement, I could see them hoist Randy up on their shoulders and march away to toast the newly crowned flyweight champion of Chapman Junior High.

Gone were my fans, my reputation and no small amount of plasma.

In a few days, when the swelling had gone down enough for me to see where I was going, I did what any nerd would do after getting an old-fashioned whupping. I went to the library. I checked out books on boxing.

In old black-and-white photos, they showed how to throw a jab, how to cross and hook, to bob and weave, to parry a punch.

I became fixated on learning to box so that I could get a rematch against Randy and reclaim my dignity. I practiced in the mirror. I persuaded my old man to get me gloves and a punching bag so I could practice on the patio. I practiced with my brother. I practiced on the cat.

I started watching boxing on TV. I got my old man to take me to the Thursday Night Fights at the Olympic Auditorium in L.A. – a classic venue, straight out of "Rocky." I stared, entranced, as these guys went head to head, magnificent athletes beating the froth out of each other on their inevitable march toward brain damage.

After several months, I decided that what I needed was a sparring partner. And I turned to one of my few remaining friends – the faithful, steadfast Spencer Kearns.

Spencer was too dorky to have very many friends in the cruel environs of junior high school. But for some reason, I had always stuck by Spencer. We had been friends since second grade. He was my buddy. And now that I was no longer popular, Spencer had stuck by me.

We strapped on gloves and went outside. I showed him how to hold his hands up in front of his face. We went to our corners, a bell rang and we came out fighting.

I jabbed twice, feigned with my right, bobbed like Joe Frazier and came lunging up with the hardest left hook I have ever thrown. I hit him smack on the chin.

When Spencer got back up, our friendship was over.

And so was my interest in boxing. Violence had gotten me nowhere. I never got my rematch with Randy Cosette. Eventually, I did get some friends back as my defeat faded away. But Spencer was done with me.

He had stuck by me, and I had repaid him by taking out all my frustration, anger and vengeance on a true friend.

Spencer, buddy, if you're out there, wherever you are, I'm sorry. It won't happen again. I'm past all that – I think.

Skiing Was More Fun When It Was Cheap

My legs are aching as I head around the track. In the fog of a January afternoon, my skin burns from the cold. In my head, a monotonous cadence clicks off the laps.

God, I hate running.

But at least I can afford running.

Most of the fun things you can do to stay in shape cost money in this day and age. Lots of money.

Either they nick you for admission, or they gouge you for equipment, or they hit you up for membership. Like health clubs, where the main exercise is craning your neck so you can see people bouncing around in outfits designed to imply sexual prowess.

And then there's skiing. I do miss skiing.

About three years ago, the ski trade press urged the industry to forget the middle class and focus on marketing to the very rich. Years of insurance hikes already had driven lift tickets to high levels. I recall gasping at $22 lift tickets. Now the prices are astronomical. This year, it's $38 for a lift ticket at most of the big Tahoe areas.

And because prices are so high, fewer and fewer people can afford to ski. So prices will have to keep going higher to make up for the lack of skiers. We could easily see $75 lift tickets this decade.

Last week I managed to get half a day in at Sierra Ski Ranch on Highway 50. I just bit the bullet and forced myself out of the office on a Friday afternoon after a couple of friends forced the issue by saying that if I didn't get out and have some fun I was setting myself up for a serious midlife crisis.

Perfect day, great snow, sunshine, friends – all the ingredients were there except one: that sense of being carefree.

The lift ticket was so high I thought they were going to insist that I show them a membership in a country club before they'd sell me one. I'm talking $21 for a half-day ticket to ski for three hours. That's only six or seven runs, at $3 per run.

I used to love skiing. Wound up becoming a Northern Californian instead of a Southern Californian because I came up here skiing one day 18 years ago and never got around to going back.

That was when skiing was what it should be: a free and easy sort of cross between sport, dance and lifestyle.

That first winter, I lived in a cabin 20 minutes away from Ski Ranch on Highway 50. Collected unemployment from a faded career as an ice-cream salesman. Took college classes. Went up to Ski Ranch three or four times a week.

It was swell. They charged about $7 for an all-day ticket, $5 for half-day. Sometimes I'd go over to Kirkwood, where they charged a couple of bucks more, but it was worth it.

Over the next decade, skiing was a big part of my life in winter. I'd sneak up three or four days a month and I'd go to the Rockies for at least a week. Skiing provided more than exercise and recreation. Because we were poor enough to have to ad lib sometimes, it provided adventure.

Like the time my friend Mike's car ran out of gas when we left Kirkwood. We were miles from the nearest station and it was getting dark. We covered some ground by pushing the car up to the top of a hill, coasting down the back of the hill, then using that momentum to push the car to the top of the next hill. That worked two or three times. But then came a big hill.

We were, in the middle of nowhere, shoving a dead car as hard as we could, and losing our last shred of momentum 150 feet from the top of the hill. Suddenly, there came a loud voice in the gathering darkness: "Are you in trouble?"

Assuming it was the voice of God, we turned around. But it was some guy who had an outside speaker mounted to his CB radio. His car had silently pulled up behind us. Happened to have a siphon hose. Despite being just married and still wearing a tuxedo, he had no objection to sucking gas for us. "Just glad it's ethyl, " he drawled, spitting out gas.

Or the time my girlfriend and I headed up in a '64 Plymouth Valiant that had carburetor and attitude problems. It had snowed all week – one of those storms where snow falls all the way down in Cameron Park. The storm cleared on Friday and we got to Kirkwood early in the morning. It was magnificent – like being in a Warren Miller powder movie. We skied all day, never stopped, and when the sun went down we spent all but our last 72 cents on a gourmet dinner in the lodge. Outside, a massive new storm was coming in.

After the last drop of wine, we trudged out to the Valiant. It wouldn't start. We went back in the bar and had the band announce that a pretty young woman and her mechanically incompetent, soon-to-be-dumped boyfriend needed help with their car. Three drunks applied for the job. I knew the Valiant would never start again when one of them pulled the distributor out of the engine, peered at it blur-rily, and announced that, "It looksh OK to me, earrrp."

We took shelter in a bar until 4 a.m., and then a local said we could sleep on the floor of his place. Except we had to use snowshoes to get to his place. When we did get home the next day, it was without the Valiant. I went back for it a week later, but it was plowed under so much snow I couldn't find it.

Then there was the time a friend and I tried to take a back road to Kirkwood because his father claimed to have taken the same short cut just the day before. "Only four inches of snow on it," his dad reported. Turned out he had taken a different back road. The one we took had four feet of snow on it. I never knew a four-wheel-drive truck could get so stuck. We didn't have a shovel, only a piece of PVC pipe to dig out with. By the time we returned to civilization, it was night.

I never laughed so hard through a crisis in all my life.

So, as I say, skiing used to be fun. But nowadays, if exercise is fun, you have to pay an arm and a leg for it.

The stingy among us run.

Straight for a midlife crisis, no doubt.

Blair's Gold Came After the '32 Olympics

A few weeks ago, the Sacramento Sports Commission announced it would be holding a banquet to honor the area's Olympic athletes. I called them, because I knew there was one athlete they probably would overlook.

The organizers were excited to learn about Bud Blair, a Placerville man who won a gold medal for rowing at the 1932 Olympics. And I was excited, too, because the banquet on May 27 would afford some recognition to a humble and worthy person.

But on the same day that 38 other Olympians and would-be Olympians gathered for a toast in Sacramento, Bud Blair died at a hospital in Placerville after being ill for less than a week. He was 82.

When I met him 16 years ago, the 1976 Olympics were about to start. I was a reporter, and somebody tipped me to him. He had rowed for UC Berkeley's crew, and in 1932, that crew had gone all the way.

I went to his tidy home in a nice, old Placerville neighborhood and knocked on the door. I recognized him from his daily walks on Main Street.

He was a tall and trim man, and there was something striking about the way he carried himself. His was not a boastful, chest-out, swaggering gait. Rather, it was simple and straight, the posture of a man still elevated by dignity at an age when most of us are being pulled down by the weight of our years.

At first, he eyed me with the suspicion that most elderly people use these days when young strangers come calling. But quickly, when he heard that I wanted to hear his story, he warmed – the way most older people do.

I entered his house, and in so doing, for a little while I entered his life. And although I was there to focus on a story about the Olympics, it quickly became apparent that those games were only an incident for James Howard Blair.

The gold medal was meaningful to him only because of what it meant to those around him. Those around him – they were the real gold.

We talked for hours. It was my intention to follow the standard interviewer's practice of having him walk me chronologically through his Olympic story. But as is often the case, the story of Bud's life was not told best in chronological order. It was a mosaic, an impressionist painting that loses its beauty when viewed too closely.

Woven through his tale of the Olympics were other tales that mattered more.

The main object on his mantel was a portrait of his wife, Gayle. She had passed away in 1972, but she was still the planetary center of his orbit. His eyes gleamed when he spoke of how she had been so proud of his Olympic scrapbooks.

Other photos of his son and daughter, and his five grandchildren and 10 great-grandchildren, adorned his walls. He told more stories about taking his grandchildren down to Cal for summertime reunions of the crew than he told about the Olympic games themselves.

When he spoke of how grueling and disciplined had been the Olympic races in the harbor at Long Beach, he drifted thoughtfully into reflections of much greater struggle and discipline in the South Pacific from 1942 to 1945. There, the medals came with malaria.

For 27 years he managed the Placerville Fruit Growers Association. He ran that office in an era when pears and apples made it one of El Dorado County's biggest companies. And the esteem in which his coworkers held him was the most important fruit of the self-confidence he had gained in his glory days of the Olympics.

This continuity, this mosaic – this was the real gold in Bud Blair's life. And what impressed me most about him was that he knew it. Most of us don't.

It shouldn't be this way, but for most of us, modern life seems to be made of separate moments, strung together like ornaments on a necklace.

Like gold medals on a ribbon.

And most of us spend our days trying to manufacture those gleaming moments. We deliberately try to create them, as if they'll provide something to look back on – something by which we can measure the meaning of our lives.

We work all week and plan weekend outings so that we can bond with our loved ones – whom we ignored all week. We save all year and go on extravagant vacations so that we'll have nice pictures for our mantels.

And somehow, we slip right through, chasing life from moment to moment. We grow too numb to covet the real gold – that which comes to us without solicitation. That which bonds the moments into a mosaic.

Moments. There's a line I heard in a song: "Like a snowflake dancing on the tip of your tongue, by the time you feel it there, it's already gone."

The Evil of Boredom in the Work Place

This just in: "Boredom tops list of reasons for business owners selling."

In any given month, half a dozen such stunning revelations come in my mail, the result of surveys conducted for our enlightenment by executive recruitment firms, business brokers and the like.

Most of the time, I don't read far beyond the first paragraph. After that, such press releases decompose into brazen sales pitches for whatever outfit sent them. That gets boring. And boredom tops the list of reasons why 90 percent of all press releases wind up in the nation's landfills.

Boredom, for that matter, tops the list of reasons why a lot of things happen. It was boredom, for example, that pushed me into journalism.

I started college right after high school but quickly grew bored and took to traveling. Alas, when the money ran out, I returned from a journey to find my parents packing a moving van. After considerable interrogation, I learned where they were moving. As a 19-year-old surfer, I did not believe in life east of the Pacific Coast Highway, so I chose not to join them in their new environs.

Thus I found myself cast upon the waters of the job market, which can be turbulent indeed when one is patently unqualified for just about every conceivable position on the planet.

The first job I landed was at McDonnell Douglas Corp. in Seal Beach. Not being qualified for the engineering department, they made me a night janitor.

My primary task at this pillar of aerospace research was to mop a moonscape of hallways. On my first night on the job, I calculated that if McDonnell Douglas simply abandoned its rocket propulsion program and set about finding a way to stack all its hallways end-to-end, we could have an American on Mars by 1973.

My second night on the job, boredom set in and I decided to get another job. On my third night on the job, they fired me, saving me from what could have been hours of excruciating deliberation. It seems my mopping skills were lacking. Some people say they are lacking to this day.

My second job was at a somewhat smaller manufacturing concern, Imperial Plastic Co., where I alone constituted the nighttime production crew. At $1.20 an hour, the wages were half what I'd made in my two-day career in aerospace, but I welcomed the challenge.

Imperial Plastic made those trays that Mother's Cookies come in. My position involved operating a vacuum machine. I fed a roll of oily plastic into the machine's bowels. Hot air wheezed into the plastic and an iron mold chomped down. All I had to do was stack the little trays as they came out four at a time.

Eight-hour graveyard shifts at Imperial Plastic were challenging enough physically, but intellectually the task proved lacking. Being the only person on the late shift provided precious few diversions, so I decided after two weeks to create a few of my own.

In the company refrigerator I found the boss's personal cellar of Mickey's Big Mouth Malt Liquor. A very short while later, the six-pack was kaput.

Time, which imparts to us great wisdom, has led me to conclude that it was probably the Mickey's Big Mouth that caused me not to notice when a bolt worked itself loose from the mold of the vacuum machine. I recall waking up when the mold bit ferociously down upon its own tongue and let out a deafening screech of pain just before it succumbed.

I never went back to collect my paycheck. To this day, I can't smell Mickey's Big Mouth without recalling the horrible scent of twisted metal and burnt plastic.

My career track was allowing me lots of time to go surfing, but it soon became difficult to buy food. One day, while pawning a guitar, I noticed a sign next door announcing immediate openings in sales – vacuum-cleaner sales.

Having had some experience with vacuums while at Imperial Plastic, I applied to be tested for the job. I soon found myself in a back room with assorted homeless people, answering questions about spatial physics: which peg goes in the round hole and so forth.

That evening, I received a buoyant call from the head vacuum cleaner salesman, informing me I'd scored highest in my class on the test and urging me to report the next morning to embark on the first day of the rest of my life, as they say in sales.

Unfortunately the surf was up the next morning, and when I called later to explain, the head vacuum salesman was rude. I was fired before boredom even set in.

The coming months brought a dizzying blur of hirings, rapidly mounting boredom, and firings characterized by a distinct lack of severance pay. I failed to make my mark as an ice-cream truck driver, a punch-press operator, a dishwasher, a retail clerk, a sign painter, and as custodian at a singles apartment complex where people were constantly straining their libidos.

I settled into doing carpentry on sailing yachts in the boatyards around Newport Beach. My proficiency grew until there existed a serious possibility that some parts of the woodwork I had done might actually survive a small Pacific storm. But again, boredom was my foe.

Being a boat builder simply wasn't panning out to be the romantic career I'd been seeking. There is, after all, something frigid about squatting beneath a $75,000 yacht, sharing your tunafish sandwich with a boatyard rat.

Unable to make an honest living, I drifted back to college and took up journalism, which had interested me in high school. And the rest, as they say, is mystery.

Journalism is hardly ever boring. And being an editor means you get to open the mail and read all those press releases based on surveys that set out to prove the obvious. And then you get to find new ways to toss them into the garbage can.

He dribbles, he fades, he jumps, he shoots.

Two points.

They Got Me – Boy Did They Get Me

Never let people who have just returned from vacation do anything important for at least a day. Don't let them make decisions. Don't let them handle complex issues. And whatever you do, don't let them negotiate so much as the purchase of paper clips.

Returning vacationers are too easily had.

Case in point: me.

It wasn't a long vacation. Just a quick week off. A little adventure south of the border. No big deal. A margarita or two, some frijoles and shrimp. I barely even relaxed.

But it was enough for me to walk back into the office gullible as a hungry halibut in a bait shop.

Unfortunately, I returned on April Fool's Day. With the wiseacres who work in this newsroom, I might as well have had a bull's eye tattooed to my forehead.

Normally, on Monday mornings the editorial staff of The Business Journal talks over the stories we're doing that week. When the meeting is over, I type a list describing the story assignments. We call it the "rundown."

So on April Fool's Day, I pull in from vacation, sickeningly cheerful. It's Tuesday morning. I need to get on top of things, so I start looking for the rundown.

Robert Celaschi, the associate editor best known for producing our "Streetwise" small-business section each week, has taken the liberty of putting this week's rundown on the seat of my chair.

He figures I will sit down on top of it and begin reading.

Which is, in a way, exactly what I do.

I glance over reporter Mark Anderson's list. It does not occur to me that a new brokerage targeting rich clients, "Butler & Nicholson," bears the names of ex-Sacramento bankers who wound up in prison.

I try to study the story list, but my mind is still being serenaded by mariachis.

I skip down to reporter Mike McCarthy's list. His top story: "Oates wants port. Offers $65 mil to buy Port of Sac, fill ship channel, build warehouses."

Geez, I think to myself, that Buzz Oates. Always doing something.

Hey, what's this? "Jim Thomas proposes Everglades theme park for waterfront, will sell marshland credits as wetland mitigation."

"Hey, McCarthy," I call out. "This story about Thomas wanting to do an Everglades theme park. Is that a scoop? Has this been reported yet?"

The entire newsroom is now aware that I have stepped into the trap. Like some Jim Carrey character, I am too stupid to see the smirks on their faces. All I see are the same expressions worn by waiters and hotel clerks in Mexico.

"Uh, no," McCarthy says. "It's an exclusive."

"Cool," I say, and skip to reporter Lynn Graebner's story list.

Her top story is about a new plan at SMUD to build "private cogen plants fueled by waste from on-site employees."

"Hey Lynn," I say. "You mean SMUD wants to build cogeneration plants fired by – by human waste?"

"Yep," she deadpans.

"Wow," I say, completely oblivious to the glee I am providing the newsroom. "Can we get a photo with that?"

The next story on Graebner's list is entitled "Bio breakthrough: Davis biotech firm engineers two-tailed crawdad."

I still don't get it.

"A two-tailed crawdad? Really?"

She is grinning fiendishly. "Yep."

"Wow," I say, my mind drifting back to lunch the day before yesterday. "That could work for lobster, too!"

"Yep," says Graebner, unable to utter more than a syllable at a time for fear she'll burst out in guffaws that could cause injury to herself and those around her.

Mentally – to the extent that any neurons are firing at all – I begin to design the front page.

We'll pair up that piece of McCarthy's about the Everglades theme park with Graebner's piece about the two-tailed crawdads, and …

Hey, wait a minute.

A light bulb goes off, very dimly, somewhere in the deep, musty folds of my cerebellum. I become aware that every lip in the room is being bitten halfway through.

I peer harder at the list.

I see that Kathy Robertson is doing a story about medical specialists committing suicide in reaction to managed care.

I see that Mark Larson is hot on a piece about Apple selling its Laguna factory to the Heaven's Gate group. And that Van Gordon Sauter is leaving KVIE to play the lead in a cable TV production of "The Burl Ives Story." And that a map of Burl Ives has been assigned to go with the article.

I see that this week's Top 25 List is going to be The Area's Largest Frivolous Lawsuits.

I see, too late to salvage any dignity whatsoever, that I have been had. Reluctantly, I lift my eyes. Everybody else, evidently, also sees that I have been had.

And so I say to you, gentle reader, that there is a lesson in all of this. We are entering the vacation season. Your bosses, employees, colleagues and clients will be returning, bleary eyed, ready to make colossal mistakes.

Don't let them. Be compassionate with them. Usher them to the lounge, sit them down and give them a crossword puzzle to work on for their first day back.

The survival of your company is at stake.